ID0788462

PAKISTAN

A PRIMARY SOURCE CULTURAL GUIDE

Marian Rengel

The Rosen Publishing Group's

New York

For my mother and father, Bernice, and Gene Rengel

Published in 2004 by The Rosen Publishing Group, Inc.
29 East 21st Street, New York, NY 10010

Copyright © 2004 by The Rosen Publishing Group, Inc.

First Edition

Library of Congress Cataloging-in-Publication Data
Rengel, Marian.
Pakistan: a primary source cultural guide/ Marian Rengel.— 1st ed.
  p. cm. — (Primary sources of world cultures)
Summary: An overview of the history and culture of Pakistan and its people including the geography, myths, arts, daily life, education, industry, and government, with illustrations from primary source documents.
Includes bibliographical references and index.
ISBN 0-8239-4001-2 (library binding)
1. Pakistan—Juvenile literature. [1. Pakistan.]
I. Title. II. Series.
DS376.9.R46 2003
954.91—dc21
                                                        2003002201

Manufactured in the United States of America

Cover images: The ruins of Mohenjo-Daro, an Indus Valley civilization dating back to the twenty-third century BC, rest atop a detail of the Indian Independence Act of 1947, which divided the nation into Hindu India and Muslim Pakistan after its independence from Great Britain. This Pakistani woman (foreground) wears traditional attire.

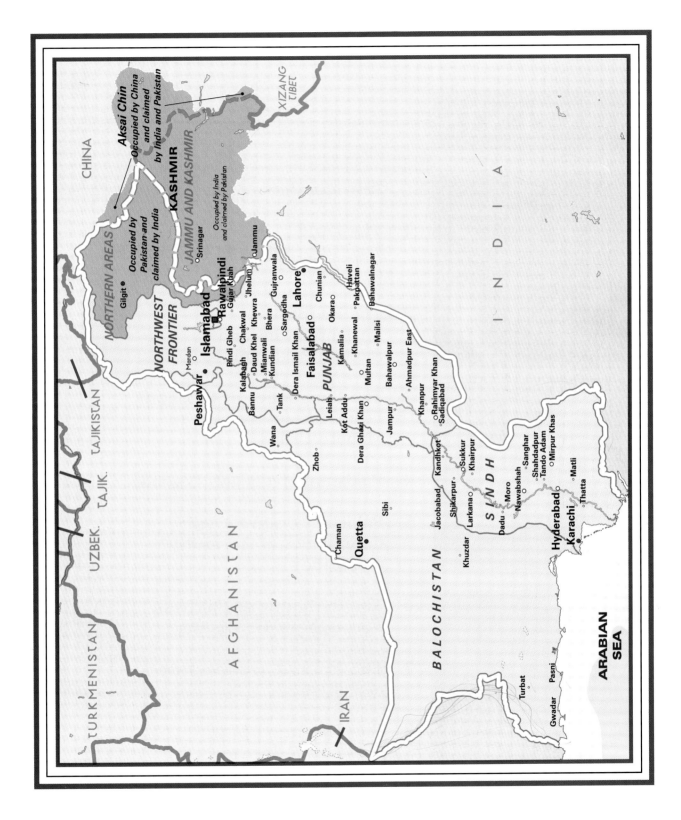

CHINA

TURKMENISTAN

UZBEK.

TAJIKISTAN

TAJIK.

AFGHANISTAN

IRAN

Aksai Chin
Occupied by China
and claimed
by India and Pakistan

NORTHERN AREAS
*Occupied by
Pakistan and
claimed by India*

Gilgit •

KASHMIR

JAMMU AND KASHMIR

*Occupied by India
and claimed by Pakistan*

XIZANG
TIBET

NORTHWEST
FRONTIER

Srinagar

Jammu

Rawalpindi
Gujar Khan

Jhelum
Gujranwala

Mardan

Islamabad

Peshawar

Pindi Gheb
Kalabagh
Bannu

Chakwal
Daud Khel
Khewra
Mianwali

Bhera
Sargodha

Lahore

Chunian
Haveli

Kundian

Okara
Kamalia
Pakpattan

Bahawalnagar

Tank

Dera Ismail Khan

Faisalabad

PUNJAB

Khanewal
Mailsi

Wana

Leiah

Kot Addu

Multan

Bahawalpur

Ahmadpur East

Dera Ghazi Khan

Jampur

Khanpur
Rahimyar Khan
Sadiqabad

Zhob

INDIA

Sibi

Chaman

Quetta

Jacobabad
Kandhkot
Shikarpur
Larkana
Khairpur
Sukkur

Khuzdar

SINDH

Dadu
Moro

Nawabshah
Sanghar
Shahdadpur
Tando Adam
Mirpur Khas
Matli

Thatta

Hyderabad
Karachi

BALOCHISTAN

Turbat

Gwadar Pasni

**ARABIAN
SEA**

CONTENTS

P akistan, a south Asian country whose name means "Land of the Pure," is a nation of contrasts. Its borders surround hot deserts and frozen glaciers, ocean shores and high mountain peaks, and both modern and traditional lifestyles.

Formally known as the Islamic Republic of Pakistan, its history as an independent nation began in 1947 when Great Britain partitioned (divided) the Indian subcontinent, which it had ruled since the mid-1800s. In granting independence to this huge territory, Great Britain accepted the demands of the millions of Muslims who had lived there since the birth of Islam, around AD 650.

When India gained independence from Great Britain in 1947, it was made into two lands: India, the large central nation, and Pakistan, which included West Pakistan and East Pakistan, one nation with two separate territories divided by the northern provinces of independent India. Only in 1971, when East Pakistan broke away from Pakistan to become the separate nation of Bangladesh, did the boundaries of today's Pakistan take form.

Hunza Valley in northern Pakistan *(left)* is situated among rugged mountains and glaciers. Visitors come to this area from May to October when the weather is warm to backpack through the valley, climb the mountains, or enjoy the villages. The four tribal clans that live in this area are all said to have originated from different regions—Dramatin from Tartary, Barataling from Russia, Kurukutz from Persia, and Broung from Kashmir. A glacier formation, located on Mount Rakaposhi in the Hunza Valley *(above)*, rises 25,551 feet (7,788 meters) above sea level. Evenings are magical as snow on Mount Rakaposhi glitters under moonlight.

Mohenjo-Daro, known as the Mound of the Dead, is an ancient city of the Harappan civilization located in the Sindh province. Built about 5,000 years ago, the square-mile city had no walls but was instead well fortified with towers to the west and south. The first excavations took place between 1922 and 1927, exposing one-third of the site. It is now believed that the settlement housed 5,000 people and had baths, assembly halls, towers, and a granary to store excess food crops.

The actual history of the land now known as Pakistan goes back thousands of years, to an ancient civilization that thrived at the same time as Mesopotamia and Egypt. Pakistan is a young nation with ancient roots.

Nomadic desert peoples and nuclear scientists, women who remain behind the veils of religious belief and soldiers who fight against India for control of Kashmir are all members of ancient ethnic tribes who proudly call themselves Pakistanis.

By 2000, there were more than 144 million people living in Pakistan. More than 97 percent of Pakistanis are Muslims, or followers of Islam. Islam is the religion of the prophet Muhammad, who first heard his calling to Allah in AD 610 and whose recitations were handed down directly from Allah. These verses now comprise the Islamic holy book known as the Koran.

With a rich history and a government that has shifted, sometimes violently, since 1947 between democracy and dictatorship, Pakistan has proven itself to be a land of contrasts.

More recently, Pakistan is a country that faces new challenges. Continued animosity between neighboring nations such as India have increased Pakistan's focus on nuclear weapons production and weapons tests that have continued in 2003. Other internal pressures include a destabilized economy made worse after foreign trade fell short of expected levels since 2001. The increased amount of foreign refugees, many of them Afghanis who made their way into Pakistan after the U.S.-led war in Afghanistan in 2002, have also been a strain on the nation's overall resources.

The Anarkali Bazaar, named for a famous courtesan of Akbar's court called Anarkali (which means "pomegranate blossom"), is located in the city of Lahore. As the city's most fascinating bazaar, it is stocked with traditional crafts, leather goods, silver, gold, and silk. The shops sell an odd mix of goods from the East and the West, everything from transistor radios to carpets, chapatis (flat breads), and chai.

THE LAND

1

The Geography and Environment of Pakistan

T he Islamic Republic of Pakistan stretches for 4,859 miles (7,820 kilometers), from some of the world's tallest mountain peaks in the north to the rocky beaches of its southern shores on the Arabian Sea.

Pakistan forms the northwestern portion of the Indian subcontinent. On its eastern border lies India, a country with which Pakistan largely shares its history. To the west lies Iran, and to the northwest, Afghanistan. China lies along Pakistan's northeastern border.

Jammu and Kashmir, a lush plateau province situated between mountain ranges in the far north and northeast of Pakistan, is also an area of conflict. Both Pakistan and India claim the province in disputes that go back to the time of Indian independence. Pakistan and India, as well as China, claim portions of this territory. A line of control, established by the United Nations in 1949 and renegotiated in 1972, now divides this region.

Pakistan, including Jammu and Kashmir, covers 307,374 square miles (796,095 square kilometers), or about twice the size of the state of California. On average, Pakistan is only about 300 miles (500 kilometers) wide, with its widest expanse in the south and its narrowest in the mountainous north.

The mountainous snow-covered Swat Valley *(left)* is known as the Switzerland of Asia. The birthplace of Tibetan Buddhism, the religion dominated the region from the second century BC, as evidenced in its many stupas and monasteries. Swat Valley was also the medieval battleground where Muslim conquerors such as Mahmud of Ghazni, Babar, and Akbar fought before moving farther into the south Asian mainland. Ogre Mountain *(above)* is part of the Karakoram Range in the Himalayas. It is a steep mountain with an elevation of 23,900 feet (7,285 meters) and whose eastern face is a sheer rock wall.

Regionally divided, Pakistan is comprised of four provinces: Baluchistan in the southwest, Sindh in the southeast, Punjab in the fertile eastern central plains, and the North-West Frontier Province (NWFP) in the mountainous western central region. These regions are very similar to the traditional lands of Pakistan's major ethnic groups: the Baluchis, Sindhis, Punjabis, Muhajirs, and Pashtuns. Though regional differences in Pakistan largely mirror ethnic distinctions, many Pakistanis live in some of the nation's largest cities, including Karachi, Islamabad, and Rawalpindi. At least a dozen cities in Pakistan have populations that exceed 200,000 residents.

Bordering Afghanistan is a region known as the Federally Administered Tribal Area, which is the responsibility of Pakistan's national government. The Islamabad Capital Territory, surrounding Pakistan's capital city of Islamabad, is also a government-controlled area.

Mountains

Four mountain ranges, including the tallest in the world, tower over northern Pakistan. The Himalayas, the Karakorams, the Hindu Kush, and the Pamirs are the result of movement of Earth's landmasses. For millions of years, the huge south Asian landmass has been sliding under the Asian continent. Pakistan, which lies on this portion of Earth's crust, frequently shakes from massive earthquakes

The Godwin-Austen Glacier is the world's second-highest mountain with an elevation of 28,250 feet (8,611 meters). Part of the Karakoram Range, it remains under Pakistani control, though portions of it fall past Pakistan's border with China. Discovered in 1856, the glacier was named after Colonel H. H. Godwin Austen, a nineteenth-century British topographer.

The Khyber Pass stretches 33 miles (53 kilometers) through the Hindu Kush and connects Pakistan with Afghanistan. It is the best regional land route and has been used by invading armies and merchants for centuries.

as a result of these movements. Together these mountains form what geologists and mountain climbers often refer to as the roof of the world.

The Himalayan Range stretches from northern Pakistan in the west to Bhutan in the east. Spurs of this great range reach across northern Pakistan and down into western Pakistan. Nanga Parbat, the world's ninth-tallest mountain, stands on the western edge of the Himalayas and overlooks the Indus River valley in southern Kashmir. Studies show that this mountain grows taller by 23 feet (7 meters) every year, making it the fastest growing mountain on Earth.

The Karakoram Range lies north of the Himalayas on the border of Pakistan and stretches for about 300 miles (483 kilometers). Its glaciers fill many of the high valleys between the spines of the mountains. The peaks of the Karakoram, such as the granite spike of Trango's Tower, are rocky, with sheer walls and towering spikes.

The world's second-highest mountain, known as K2 or Mount Godwin-Austen, stands 28,250 feet (8,611 meters) tall, just slightly lower than Mount Everest in Nepal. Its northern side reaches into China, and its southern side reaches into Pakistan-controlled Kashmir.

Sitting between Pakistan and Afghanistan are the mountains of the Hindu Kush. As far back as ancient times, perpetually snow-covered passes through this mountain range allowed people from central Asia to invade the south Asia subcontinent. These lower mountains, which form much of Pakistan's western landscape, reach only as high as 18,000 feet (5,550 meters), much lower in comparison to peaks in the Himalayas and the Karakoram, but taller than the Rocky Mountains in North America.

North of Pakistan, across a narrow portion of Afghanistan, sits the Pamir Range. Its edges touch northern Pakistan and blend into the Himalayas, the Hindu Kush, and the Karakoram.

The ancient city of Mohenjo-Daro was built according to a grid pattern with parallel streets, which crossed each other to divide the city into blocks. There was also an advanced drainage system through the streets to keep the area sanitary. Historians believe that the civilization ended 3,700 years ago when the Indus River changed its course.

Deserts

A desert dominated by arid conditions largely covers Pakistan, especially the western half of the nation. Strong winds blow the sands of the Thar Desert, also known as the Great Indian Desert, between Pakistan and India. A border through this 77,000-square-mile (200,200-square-kilometer) region puts about one-third of the desert in Pakistan and the rest in India with winds blowing so strong that the desert often buries nearby lands.

In Pakistan, the northern part of the Thar, in the province of Punjab, is known as the Cholistan. Here the ruins of Mohenjo-Daro, the ancient Indus Valley civilization that thrived from about 2500 to 1500 BC, can be found. The southeastern tip of Pakistan and the edge of this desert become part of the Rann of Kutch, a saltwater swamp found mostly in India that dries into a cracked mud flat during the dry season.

Sandy deserts and cactus-covered hills make up much of Baluchistan, the name of the western province of Pakistan and a larger geographic region that stretches into neighboring Iran.

In central Pakistan, on the eastern side of the Sulaiman Range of the Hindu Kush and the eastern banks of the Indus River, stretches the Thal Desert, also known as the Indus Valley Desert. The second most desolate area of Pakistan, this 7,500-square-mile (19,500-square-kilometer) region experiences extreme temperatures and less than 3 inches (8 centimeters) of rain each year.

Rivers

The Indus River has brought life to India and the region that is now Pakistan for thousands of years. High in the Himalayan Mountains of Tibet in a lake near Mount Kailas, the Indus begins its 1,900-mile (3,060-kilometer) journey to the Arabian Sea. Fed by mountain snowmelt, it picks up the waters of small tributaries and one major river, the Shyok, before turning southwest and flowing into the heartland of Pakistan. In its delta, the river passes through a great mangrove forest, which removes much of the salt from the water before it enters the Arabian Sea.

In Pakistan, four rivers, the Jhelum, Chenab, Ravi, and Sutlej, and their maze of tributaries and canals join with the Indus. This network of waterways, with areas between the streams known as *doabs*, provides agricultural irrigation to Pakistan's main regions and water for Punjab, its most heavily populated province. The Indus is one of the most heavily dammed rivers in the world. Pakistanis divert the waters of the Indus and Jhelum Rivers for farming and urban needs. Most recently, the power of the Indus,

A tractor maneuvers through the flooded streets of Rawalpindi after a severe downpour in July 2001. Several houses were washed away in the twin cities of Rawalpindi and Islamabad after receiving a record 24.4 inches (62 cm) of rain.

A man rows a small boat on the Indus River, a waterway that extends from the Himalayas to the Arabian Sea. Since most of Pakistan is arid, the Indus serves a vital role in the country. It irrigates 80 percent of Pakistan's farmland through canals.

known in ancient Indian works as the King River, is being harnessed as a source for Pakistan's electrical power needs.

Climate

Pakistan stretches through three regions, each with its own distinct climate. In the north are mountain highlands, in the central region are semiarid plains, and in the south is desert.

In the mountains, Pakistan's climate is cool and temperate in the summer and cold and snowy in the winter, while the desert is hot and dry all year long. Only the heavy rains of monsoon season—from July through September—bring some relief from the desert heat in the south.

While some people say that Pakistan has two seasons, hot and wet, climate experts divide its year into three seasons: cool in winter (October through February); hot in spring (March through June); and wet in summer (July through September).

This view of the financial district in downtown Karachi shows one of Pakistan's most populated areas. It is composed of a combination of narrow, twisting lanes of the old city along with modern buildings and highways. The history of Karachi dates from the eighteenth century when it was a fishing village called Kalachi-jo-Goth.

Flora and Fauna

More than 180 species of mammals, 150 species of reptiles, 600 species of birds, and 150 species of fish, as well as hundreds of species of insects and amphibians, live in Pakistan.

High in the northern mountains lives the *markhor*, a member of the goat family with broad spiraling horns and a shaggy, long beard. Marco Polo sheep, the largest species of sheep, live high in the mountains, too.

Pakistan is home to three recently endangered species: the Indus River dolphin, the snow leopard, and the woolly flying squirrel. Another eight of its animals are close to being classified as endangered.

Many small mammals, such as mice and voles, make their homes in the deserts of Pakistan. Some of its larger mammals include wolves, hyenas, and leopards. In the mountainous northern regions live Asiatic black bears, leopards, wild sheep, Asiatic ibex, wild dogs, and goats.

Among Pakistan's permanent avian are golden eagles, peregrine falcons, well-camouflaged sand grouses, cuckoos, and woodpeckers. Poachers and hunters in Pakistan threaten the Houbara bustard almost to the point of extinction.

Common flora in Pakistan includes pine forests that grow in high mountain regions. Oak, maple, alder, and walnut trees grow in the mid-mountain ranges. Mangrove trees live off the salt in the water of the Indus River delta and provide homes to many fish and aquatic species such as frogs, snakes, and flamingos.

One of the world's largest remaining juniper forests stretches across the north-central region of the Baluchistan plateau. Almond, walnut, and pistachio trees also fill open woodlands in this western region. Jasmine, Pakistan's national flower, grows lushly in the foothills of the Himalayas. Many flowers native to this region have names familiar to gardeners in North America: rhododendron, gentian, poppy, anemone, honeysuckle, and sage, many of which were imported to North America from Asia in the 1800s.

The Houbara bustard is a small desert bird that inhabits arid areas. These birds feed on insects, lizards, and seeds, and are well camouflaged while at rest.

THE PEOPLE

2

Ancient Aryans and Modern Pakistanis

A ncient civilizations have brought diversity to Pakistan. Some Pakistanis trace their origins to the Indus Valley civilization of 2500 BC, while others are linked to Africans who found their way centuries ago to Pakistan's Arabian coast. Many conquerors and empires have also colored Pakistan's rich history, making it an ethnically diverse nation of people.

The Indus Valley Civilization

In the 1920s, archaeologists discovered evidence near the Indus River of a sophisticated empire that flourished about 4,500 years ago. They found ruins of two great cities, which they called Harappa and Mohenjo-Daro. Kot Diji, yet another important archaeological site—but one that predates both Harappa and Mohenjo-Daro—has been found in Pakistan's Sindh province. Historians knew very little about these

ancient peoples except that they had been mentioned in Buddhist documents.

The Indus Valley civilization, also known as the Harappan civilization, thrived from 2500 to 1600 BC. Its people used a form of writing that scientists have not yet deciphered, so information about the culture has been limited to what may be determined from its artifacts. People of the Indus Valley made small squares that they used as seals, engraved clay that was impressed by stamps. Archaeologists have found thousands of

The Kot Diji Fort *(left)* is a Pakistani national monument. Its discovery provides evidence that settlements in the country later known as Pakistan existed before those of Harappa and Mohenjo-Daro, possibly between 2500 and 2800 BC. Excavations have proven that the Indus Valley civilizations borrowed some of the basic elements from the Kot Dijians. Cubed dice *(above)* found at Mohenjo-Daro date from 3000 to 2000 BC.

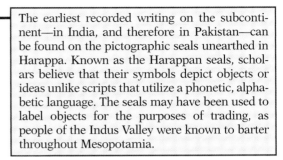

The earliest recorded writing on the subcontinent—in India, and therefore in Pakistan—can be found on the pictographic seals unearthed in Harappa. Known as the Harappan seals, scholars believe that their symbols depict objects or ideas unlike scripts that utilize a phonetic, alphabetic language. The seals may have been used to label objects for the purposes of trading, as people of the Indus Valley were known to barter throughout Mesopotamia.

these small squares imprinted with human and animal images. Recent excavations in these cities, which may have been home to more than 80,000 people, also revealed that its people made jewelry.

The Indus Valley people were farmers, artisans, and traders. They grew enough food for their needs, but they also became wealthy through their trading contacts with people throughout Asia and the Middle East. Archaeologists have enough evidence to prove that people of the Indus Valley domesticated animals, stored excess crops, minted copper, and organized their cities in grid patterns. Archaeological evidence also shows that this society developed a primitive form of weights and measures, as well as constructed a system for water drainage. Even so, scientists do not know what caused this civilization to end so abruptly. By 1500 BC, its people perhaps abandoned their cities for a more nomadic lifestyle.

This ancient statue of a high priest was unearthed in the 1920s from the archaeological site of Mohenjo-Daro. One of the earliest known cities in the world, its inhabitants were known to have worshiped many different gods and goddesses as well as animals.

The Vedic Civilization

Around 1500 BC, many nomadic tribes from central Asia known as Aryans (Indo-Europeans) crossed the mountains and entered India from the northwest. They arrived in the region later known as Pakistan, and, according to ancient records, intermixed with the people living around the Indus Valley. The Aryans' former homeland was located between the Black and the Caspian Seas in western Asia and eastern Europe.

The Aryans were a warlike people who harbored little of the sophistication of the former Indus settlements. Initially without language, the Aryans were a tribal people who conquered inhabitants near the Ganges floodplain, where they eventually concentrated. Unlike earlier settlements, however, the Aryans did not build elaborate cities. Their tribal community was organized in individual units called *jana* or *jati*, which

Recent Archaeological Evidence

Baluchistan, Pakistan, is the home of some of the world's most important recent archaeological discoveries, including the dinosaur fossils seen in this photograph. During the 1990s, archaeologists battled seasonal flooding in the Greater Hab River valley, as well as the plain of Las Bela, to find some of the world's oldest known settlements, some of which predate the Indus Valley civilizations by 8,000 years. Stripping away years of silt remains, archaeologists found evidence of settlements once populated by people who carved stone and clay artifacts. Although the search of the area is ongoing, current sites are located in Las Bela (composed of several settlements including Adam Buthi, Niai Buthi, and Balakot). As far as scientists can tell, Las Bela fell into a mysterious decline and was finally void of occupants around 3000 BC.

The Drokpa woman in this photograph is praying. The Drokpas are a small community of pure Aryans who live in the restricted area of northern Ladakh bordering Pakistan. As Buddhists, the Drokpas make a pilgrimage to Tabo to attend the Kalachakra ceremony performed by the fourteenth Dalai Lama.

were ruled by one warrior. The Aryans, like the Indians after them, divided their society according to specific social classes, much as India's later caste system. The Aryans did have a well-developed musical culture, however, which probably assisted in their development of spoken poetry and, later, a written script.

Aryan warriors largely dominated the subcontinent for centuries. Many remained in the northwestern plateaus and in the Indus River valley, passing their traditions to their Indian descendants.

The Vedic period (1500 BC to 200 BC) is important because the four Vedas, or Books of Knowledge, were developed during this time. Handed down from generation to generation, the Vedas were eventually written in Sanskrit, India's official language of literature. The first text of the Vedas, the Rig Veda, contains hymns about nature and gods. The other three books are known as the Sama Veda, a book of mantras, or mystical phrases; the Yajureda, a book of mystical formulas; and the Atharva Veda, which contains ancient medical prescriptions. The Vedas were considered divinely inspired

Modern editions of the four Vedas, pictured in this contemporary photograph, are written in Sanskrit, the literary language of India. The Vedas each contain four distinct parts: the mantra or hymn, which is the earliest text known as *samhita*; a text for Hindu teaching (*brahmana*); a section about theology (*aranyaka*); and a section about philosophy (*upanishads*). The Vedas were first compiled around 3500 BC.

and eventually became the cornerstone of all Indian knowledge.

The Persians

As the Aryans grew stronger, they became targets of invaders. During the sixth century BC, Cyrus the Great, king of Persia (Iran), crossed the Hindu Kush and conquered the Aryan people. He established four provinces of his empire in the Indus River valley, including Gandhara, the land now situated around Peshawar.

Cyrus the Great is often remembered for being a diplomat as well as a conqueror because he freed the Hebrews after his conquest of Babylon, sending them to Palestine. Although Cyrus himself worshiped a religion established by the Persians called Zoroastrianism (founded by Zarathustra during the seventh century BC), he was respectful of other religions, too. Although the extent of Cyrus's conquests are not known, he did establish three capitals, Susa, Ecbatana, and Babylon, and he paved the way for the

This stone carving of Cyrus the Great as a genie with four wings was discovered in Pasargadae, the ancient capital city of Persia. The sculpture is the oldest intact Achaemenid bas-relief and reflects Cyrus's dedication to the philosophy of multiculturalism. Cyrus was the first-known king to create policies that called for the peaceful cohabitation of people from various cultures.

The Birth of Buddhism

Siddhartha Gautama, later known as the Buddha, or the "one who knows," was born into a wealthy royal family in 563 BC in Nepal. Influenced by the pain and suffering that he saw in the feebleness and poverty of strangers, he soon questioned the root of human misery. In order to understand the pain felt by others, the Buddha searched for answers to the reasons for the world's suffering. Soon he renounced his material possessions and learned to meditate. Eventually he received a vision of enlightenment, a state often referred to as nirvana.

Buddhism grew steadily in the first few centuries after its birth, at first spread by the Indian king Asoka who adopted the religion during his reign in the third century BC. Asoka subscribed to Buddhist beliefs and spread its message of nonviolence, ordering a series of pillars inscribed with his edicts, or decrees.

The rapid popularity of Buddhism was based on its overall appeal, humane outlook, and emphasis on social renewal. Over the centuries, there has been an exchange of ideas between Hinduism and Buddhism. For instance, the Hindu ideals of vegetarianism and *ahimsa* (nonviolence) originated from Buddhism, and Buddha is one of the incarnations of Vishnu, a popular Hindu god.

Persian empire. Cyrus was buried in a tomb at Pasargadae in 529 BC, where he had built a beautiful palace.

Gandhara would later become a center of artistic, religious, and economic development that would thrive for more than 500 years despite frequent invasions and changes in leadership.

The Greeks

Alexander the Great, Macedonian conqueror of a vast empire, pushed his army into south Asia, crossing the Hindu Kush in 327 BC. For nearly three years, his soldiers fought

Alexander the Great, king of Macedonia, accomplished greater conquests than any leader before him, but because he did not construct governments in any of the lands he conquered, his territories were never united as one empire. Although he was an unsuccessful politician, he was one of the greatest military leaders of all time. His influence spread Greek culture, known as Hellenism, which helped establish city-states modeled after Greek institutions.

to conquer the northwest kingdoms of the subcontinent. Ruins of a mud fort built by Alexander in Sindh still mark the eastern edge of his empire.

As Alexander's armies moved eastward, colonists followed, bringing with them their Hellenistic (Greek) arts, architecture, and culture. This Hellenistic style influenced the development of Indian Buddhist sculpture in two Buddhist cities: Gandhara and Mathura. This influence on art, now known as the Gandharan period, flourished between the first and seventh centuries AD in the area that would later become Pakistan. The first time that the Buddha was represented in human form was during this period.

After Alexander's death in 323 BC, his empire crumbled and was divided among his generals. Many Greek citizens remained in the region, however, adding their influence to its culture.

The Birth of Islam

Islam began when Muhammad, known as the Prophet, first began hearing the words of the archangel Gabriel in Arabia during the sixth century AD. The word "Islam" is Arabic and means "submission [to Allah]." Muhammad's messages—believed by Muslims to have come directly from Allah—are collected in the Islamic holy book known as the Koran. Islam spread to India by way of early converts—merchants and traders—but mostly through forced military campaigns. Other people were Hindus who saw conversion to Islam as a way to rise from the low status of their caste.

By AD 711, Muhammad bin Qasim, an army general from Damascus, an ancient city now in Iraq, attacked the southern shores of Sindh. This army was part of the rapidly growing Arab Empire, the new followers of Islam. After defeating the nearby port city, Qasim destroyed a Buddhist holy site and built the first mosque on the continent.

درختهای انار هم هست کردا کرد حوض تمام سبزکزار

بای غین باغ همین است در وقت زرد شدن باز به جهای بسیار

Islam replaced the idea of idol worship and was then, as it is now, a monotheistic religion. India was gradually infused with an entirely new Islamic culture that included architecture, language, cuisine, and attire.

Thousands of Arab settlers followed the army to the Indian peninsula. Over six centuries, conversions and conquests spread Islam over a region that was once dominated by Buddhists and Hindus. It wouldn't be until the fourteenth century, however, that Muslim invaders formed a stable government, beginning with the Mughal Empire of Babur.

The Mughal Empire

In 1398, the first of the great Mughal warrior leaders invaded the Indus Valley. The origins of the Mughal people are unknown. They appear to be Mongol descendants of Genghis Khan, who in the early 1220s became a powerful conqueror, establishing the

Mongol Empire, which stretched from eastern China into Persia (Iran), Mesopotamia (Iraq), and parts of northern Asia. The Mughals most likely settled in the mountains of what is now Tajikistan.

Babur (1483–1530)—known as the Tiger—a Mughal conqueror and ruler of Kabul, now in Afghanistan, took his armed troops across the Hindu Kush and into the plains east of the Indus River in 1504. Once there, he began his quest to unite the many small kingdoms of India under his rule.

With military success and cooperation from local rulers, Babur built the Mughal Empire. Babur's son Humayun (1508–1556) took his place in 1530, but was not as enlightened as his father and had little love for learning. Babur is remembered for introducing the empire to the arts and language of Persia. Under his reign, Persian became the official language of all court poetry. Following Humayun, the leadership of Akbar

This watercolor painting from the *Baburnama (left)* dates from 1589 and depicts Babur supervising the Garden of Fidelity. The *Baburnama*, Babur's book of memoirs, recorded the events during his reign from 1494 to his death in 1530. It also celebrates his love of nature. Gardens closely represent the concept of paradise in Islam, often described as beautiful places that include foliage, fountains, and rivers. A painting *(above)* depicts the Mughal emperor Akbar the Great entering Surat in 1572. Akbar realized that Hindu acceptance and cooperation were required to successfully rule any conquered country. He extended his realm by conquest until it spread from Afghanistan to the Bay of Bengal and from the Himalayas to the Godavari River.

(1542–1605) firmly established the empire artistically in terms of its architecture, carefully constructed communities, and lavish gardens, finally moving its capital to Lahore. During its years of decline, the Mughal Empire was ruled by Jahangir (1605–1627), his son Shah Jahan (1592–1666), and finally Aurangzeb (1618–1707).

The British

Merchants from England arrived in India during the reign of Queen Elizabeth I, in the late 1500s, shortly after Vasco da Gama discovered a sea route to India for the Europeans in 1498. The British sought the riches of Asia, which included spices, jewels, and silk. The East India Company, an English trading firm formed in 1600, established trade routes and relationships with the Indian people. Eventually, British leaders forced the French from India in 1757 and used military and political power to gain increased access to its land and resources. Soon British leaders began the political process of making India part of its imperial empire, which, at the time, also included lands in North America.

At first working through the East India Company, and finally taking direct control of the country, Great Britain became the sovereign ruler of India during the reign of Queen Victoria. Many Muslims see this occupation as a strain on their culture because British India became highly Westernized. British inhabitants quickly alienated

This illustration from 1812 depicts Bombay Green in India during 1767. The private army of the East India Company drills on the green. India was often called the British Empire's "Crown Jewel" largely because of the company's success. It employed a private army to protect its factory in India's often-hostile environment. The use of force to support British commerce in India was commonplace, and the private company army eventually rivaled the British army in manpower.

Muhammad Ali Jinnah

Muhammad Ali Jinnah was so important to providing a nation for the Muslims of south Asia that Pakistanis call him Quaid-e-Azam, meaning leader of the nation. Jinnah, once a successful lawyer, believed very strongly in the rights of Muslims. During his lifetime, he was able to persuade the Muslims of then British India that they deserved their own homeland.

Jinnah was born on December 25, 1876, in Karachi, the son of a well-to-do merchant. After many years of schooling—both in India and abroad—he established a law practice in Bombay (Mumbai). He entered politics in 1905, advocating for an independent India. As a Muslim, Jinnah saw the conflict between Muslims and Hindus; the Hindus held more government jobs and had better access to education and opportunities than did Muslims.

As a lawyer, Jinnah joined the Muslim League in 1913 and worked hard to improve resources for Indian Muslims. Members of this group supported efforts to increase the political voices of Muslims in India. Struggles between different political groups in India, however, led to great conflict between religious groups. Jinnah and others concluded that for Muslims to have the opportunity for education and better jobs, they would need to separate from the Hindu majority in India's regional government. Jinnah realized that if Great Britain were to grant independence in south Asia, it would need to make two separate nations.

By 1934, Jinnah became the leader of the Muslim League and campaigned across British India for a new Muslim nation. He also worked to persuade leaders that they needed to form two nations when they stopped ruling this land. After much work, Jinnah was successful in his efforts to create the independent nation of Pakistan and became its first governor-general in 1947. Sadly, he died just one year later, in 1948.

This portrait of Queen Victoria (1819–1901), a monarch often associated with England's Industrial Age, dates from 1886. She was influenced by her first prime minister Lord Melbourne and her husband, Prince Albert, both of whom taught her how to be a more effective ruler.

Muslims, who, compared to Hindus, were never given an equal education or equal opportunities.

The Struggle for Independence

During the 1940s and before, Muslims had wanted their own nation. They wanted the provinces governed by Great Britain, that were largely home to Muslims, to become a separate Muslim nation. Most of the people in the other provinces on the peninsula belonged to the Hindu religion and also wanted a separate nation.

By 1946, these religious disagreements about beliefs and political representation erupted into violent outbursts. Thousands of people—both Hindus and Muslims—died during this struggle and civil discord.

Before the independence of India, Pakistan was known as an Islamic republic. In 1956, the Islamic Republic of Pakistan, which was split into East Pakistan and West Pakistan, developed a new constitution. Millions of people fled to opposite borders after partition—August 14–15—the term for the separation of Pakistan from India, creating chaos, turmoil, and violence across south Asia. (By 1971, East Pakistan became the independent country of Bangladesh.) That same year (1971), India joined with Bangladesh and entered into a war with Pakistan, which was soon defeated, costing about one million lives. Now smaller and with a decreased population, Pakistan established a new leader, Prime Minister Zulfikar Ali Bhutto, who reigned over the nation until 1977.

Bhutto created Pakistan's new constitution in 1973 and addressed some of the nation's most vital needs, including improved health care and educational systems. His reign of power was darkened by corruption, however, when in the late 1970s, allegations of rigged elections became well known.

In 1977, Bhutto was placed under house arrest by General Muhammad Zia-ul-Haq who then ruled Pakistan for ten years, reducing corruption and restoring order.

The Indian National Congress struggled for the independence of all Indian provinces, including British India, Indian states, French India, and Portuguese India. The British passed the Indian Independence Act in 1947, granting freedom to British Indian provinces and Indian states. This act created India and Pakistan, and ended Britain's control over Indian affairs beginning August 15, 1947. Pakistan thus became an independent state.

Section.

An Act to make provision for the setting up in India of two independent Dominions, to substitute other provisions for certain provisions of the Government of India Act, 1935, which apply outside those Dominions, and to provide for other matters consequential on or connected with the setting up of those Dominions.

[18th July 1947.]

BE it enacted by the King's most Excellent Majesty, by and with the advice and consent of the Lords Spiritual and Temporal, and Commons, in this present Parliament assembled, and by the authority of the same, as follows :—

1.—(1) As from the fifteenth day of August, nineteen hundred and forty-seven, two independent Dominions shall be set up in India, to be known respectively as India and Pakistan. *The new Dominions.*

(2) The said Dominions are hereafter in this Act referred to as "the new Dominions", and the said fifteenth day of August is hereafter in this Act referred to as "the appointed day".

2.—(1) Subject to the provisions of subsections (3) and (4) of this section, the territories of India shall be the territories under the sovereignty of His Majesty which, immediately before the appointed day, were included in British India except the territories which, under subsection (2) of this section, are to be the territories of Pakistan. *Territories of the new Dominions.*

(2) Subject to the provisions of subsections (3) and (4) of this section, the territories of Pakistan shall be—

(a) the territories which, on the appointed day, are included in the Provinces of East Bengal and West Punjab, as constituted under the two following sections ;

Although Pervez Musharraf—Pakistan's president and chief executive—was born in India, he and his family were among the first to relocate to the newly independent Pakistan in 1947. He took control of the country in 1999, was made its president in 2001, and was elected to a seven-year term in 2002.

Zia-ul-Haq accused Bhutto of ordering the murder of a political opponent prior to elections. Soon after promising free elections, Zia-ul-Haq died in an unexplained plane crash. Bhutto was later found guilty of corruption and was executed.

By 1985, a newer version of Pakistan's constitution was adopted; one that allowed strict elections. Three years later, Benazir Bhutto, the daughter of the former prime minister, was chosen to head Pakistan. Again faulted for corruption, Benazir Bhutto was disposed of in 1990, then living in exile in England. New elections brought Nawaz Sharif to power. In 1999, General Pervez Musharraf took control of the nation in a bloodless coup and became its head of government. The people of Pakistan affirmed his rule in a referendum held in 2001.

Modern Ethnic Groups

For centuries, Muslims ruled India. However, under British rule, many Muslims followed strict Islamic laws and refused to learn English. They did not wish to become a part of the modernizing forces sweeping the subcontinent.

Muslims of various ethnic groups began their struggle for independence in the late 1800s. When Great Britain decided to give India its independence in the 1940s, Muslim leaders persuaded the British to divide the subcontinent into two nations—India, and a Muslim homeland separate from the Hindu nation.

Pakistan became that Muslim nation in 1947. A portrait of Pakistan before 1971 would have included the Bengali people of East Pakistan, but after the formation of Bangladesh in that year, Pakistan became a land of five distinct ethnic groups.

The Baluchi

Most of the nearly five million Baluchi people of Baluchistan live seminomadic lives in the mountains of western Pakistan. These independent herders and farmers trace their ancestry to an uncle of the prophet Muhammad, founder

This photograph of a Baluchi woman was taken during her journey to Firuzabad, a town on the border between Pakistan and Iran. The Baluchis have inhabited the remote mountains and desert regions of Pakistan for more than 1,000 years. Today, Pakistan's Baluchi population totals approximately 5 million people.

of Islam, and to those who came originally from Syria.

The Baluchi respect bravery and courage, traits honored in their folk songs. They also honor their tribal heroes in the Baluchi Way, a traditional code of honor and proper conduct. Though most Baluchis are Muslims, the tribes within this culture follow tribal social customs rather than Islamic law. Many Baluchis maintain beliefs that their people held before Islam, such as the influences of their ancestors' spirits over their lives.

Poets and musicians are treasured by Baluchi, who have a strong oral tradition of poetry and folktales. Baluchi men often wear their hair and beards long, dress in white robes, and don long turbans known as *pags*.

The Muhajir

While not an ethnic group based on ancestry and a traditional homeland, Muhajir (a word meaning "refugee"; also known as Mohajir) are Muslims who immigrated to Pakistan at the time of Indian independence.

These people, fearing oppression from Hindus who did not want the separation of the nation, fled into Pakistan. Muhajir are generally well educated and once held positions of responsibility in the provinces that they left, leading a majority heading to Karachi, as well as other cities. Muhajir struggled to retain their traditions and language, Urdu. Historically, much violence has been expressed toward Muhajir, especially since they assumed many prominent positions once held by Indian Hindus. Today Pakistan is home to about eleven million Muhajirs.

The Punjabi

The people of Punjabi ancestry represent the majority, or about 60 percent, of Pakistan's population. Most live in the agricultural areas of northern and central Punjab, the most prosperous portion of Pakistan. Punjabi appear to be descendents of Aryans. The traditional Punjabi homeland stretched across the Indus River valley from the current western border of Punjab province to Delhi, a major city in northwestern India.

Modern influences are changing the traditions of the Punjabi people. More than half live in Pakistan's cities, earning their living in prominent positions in government, industry, and medicine.

Other more traditional Punjabi are farmers who make their living working the fields. Many own their own land. This smaller percentage of Punjabi live in small, close-knit communities. Punjabi traditional dress for men usually includes a long outer cloth wrap called a *dhoti*, as well as a turban. A Punjabi woman usually wears a long shirt that is known as the *salwar kameez* and a veil called a *dupatta*.

The Pashtun

About thirteen million Pashtun (also known as Pakhtun, Pathan, and Pushtun) live in Pakistan, most in the North-West Frontier Province. For generations, the mountain passes of west central Pakistan and eastern Afghanistan have allowed invaders access to the Indian subcontinent, the same region that is now home to Pashtun tribes. During the nineteenth century, Pashtun ruthlessly fought for control of the Khyber Pass from invading British soldiers, who claimed these tribal people were among the most passionate fighters in all of south Asia. Besides living in an area known as the crossroads of great civilizations, the Pashtun claim ancestry primarily from Afghana, a grandson of King Saul of Israel.

Pashtun are rugged, warlike people who find identity in their tribes. Members of a clan or tribe will often trace their descent to common male ancestors. A tribal council oversees daily life and maintains social order in Pashtun society by following a specific

Pashtuns, like the man seen in this photograph, are the Pashtu-speaking people of Afghanistan and northwestern Pakistan. Pashtun society revolves around a strict code of ethics. It is an unwritten code that includes hospitality, right of blood feuds, revenge, bravery, and the defense of women and property. The Pashtun are among Pakistan's largest ethnic groups.

code of living called *Pukhtunwali*. The main ideal of this code is to act honorably at all times. Respecting the elder tribal members, especially the men who hold the most authority, is very important to Pashtun. They also believe that any member of a tribe who seeks shelter or sanctuary should receive unconditional protection. This idea is called *melmastia*.

Pashtuns are an agricultural and nomadic people, though many have moved into cities and found careers. Folktales tell stories of tribal relationships, friendships, and love affairs. Traditional Pashtun clothes are often highly embroidered.

The Sindhi

The Sindhis, inhabitants of Pakistan's rural Sindh province, are direct descendants of people who have lived in this desert region for many generations, possibly including those who once inhabited the ancient Indus Valley civilization. Sindhi are known for their mystical religious poetry and music.

Today's twenty million Sindhi are largely Muslim, but their culture has been highly influenced by Hinduism. Families are organized into *zats*, hereditary occupational groups, where people are born into the type of jobs and careers they are allowed to have for their entire lives, similar to the practice of India's caste system. Modern Sindhi live in Karachi, though most are desert farmers, growing wheat where the waters of the Indus irrigate the desert.

The oldest man is the head of a Sindhi family, and women—who are not allowed in public uncovered—run the household. Women must raise children from within the village or home. This tradition is changing for modern Sindhi women. Benazir Bhutto, a woman who was elected twice as Pakistan's prime minister, is Sindhi.

The Sindhi people are named after the Sindu (Indus) River and are said to be one of Pakistan's oldest groups. Today, many Sindhi, such as this man, work in irrigation farming, while others raise livestock. Some live in cities and work as merchants, doctors, lawyers, and teachers. Traditionally, Muslim Sindhi women stay at home, leaving only to visit family members and the local mosque.

THE LANGUAGES OF PAKISTAN

3

From Ancient Sanskrit to Modern Urdu

M any languages and dialects are currently spoken throughout Pakistan, many of them dividing the nation regionally, such as along the borders of its four separate provinces. And though these variations contribute to Pakistan's cultural differences, most Pakistanis are bilingual, which means that they can read and write in two languages. Since the majority of Pakistanis are also Muslim, they frequently memorize passages from the Koran, which is written in Arabic.

From the official language of Urdu to rare languages spoken by fewer than 200 people, Pakistan is home to approximately sixty-five different languages. Pakistan's diversity of language comes, in part, from India's rich history of invasion and conquest.

Since Pakistan was partitioned from India in 1947, much has been said about its need for a national language. Today, many Pakistanis are part of an ongoing language movement that opposes the nationalization of both Urdu and English. As Muslims, some Pakistanis feel that a more appropriate national language should have been Arabic, the language of the Koran. Others feel that Farsi, the contemporary Persian, would be more appropriate, since it was once the literary language of the Mughals, expanded by their empire throughout Asia during the sixteenth and seventeenth centuries. Most eastern Islamic kingdoms between the ninth and thirteenth centuries adopted a classical form of Persian.

This horse-drawn carriage *(left)* travels the road between Islamabad and Peshawar below a wall of advertising signs in various languages. A man *(above)* reads a Pakistani newspaper. The national language of Pakistan is Urdu, but few people use it as their first language. Punjabi is the most widely spoken language in the country, followed by Sindhi, Pashtu, and Saraiki. English is also an official language in Pakistan, though it is mostly used by government officials.

This young boy from Lahore is studying the Koran. Throughout Pakistan, religious schools called *madrassas* offer free instruction in Islamic studies for students ages eight to fifteen. Students who attend madrassas are required to memorize verses of the Koran and to learn how to live a pure Islamic life. There are separate schools for boys and girls, and they are often attached to individual mosques.

Nearly all of Pakistan's languages are of Indo-European origin, which means that people living in areas from northern India to eastern Europe took part in their development. The modern languages that grew from those beginnings include English, French, Italian, Russian, and many others. All around the world people speak at least one of the more than seventy-eight living Indo-European languages.

More specifically, the languages of Pakistan belong to the Indo-Iranian subfamily of the Indo-European group. This subfamily is divided into the Indo-Aryan (also known as Indic) and Iranian languages.

Urdu

Urdu, a language that originated during the Mughal period, has been the official language of Pakistan since 1988. The name Urdu literally means "a camp language" because it was spoken originally by Mughal troops. Urdu was later adopted by local speakers who mixed it with Hindi words and dialects. It is now a language recognized as one of the fifteen official languages of India, simplifying communication between the two neighboring nations. It is of Indo-Aryan descent and was once the language of upper-class Muslim families living in northern India prior to its independence. Many people consider Urdu the written or literary form of Hindustani, a common language once used by many Muslims. Urdu is actually a mixture of Persian, Arabic, and various local languages, and is similar to Hindi, one of the official languages of India. During the 1970s, riots broke out by protesting Bengalis in East Pakistan (present-day Bangladesh) who did not wish to adopt Urdu. The Bengalis of Bangladesh now speak Bengali.

Urdu is the mother tongue of about eleven million Pakistanis, or about 8 percent of the population of Pakistan. Still another 10 percent know Urdu as their second language. In 1973, the Pakistani constitution set standards for replacing English with Urdu as the official language of Pakistan by 1988.

People use variations of Arabic letters to write Urdu. Great works of poetry have been written in Urdu, some of it by Pakistani authors, some by Indian authors, and some by people who wrote long before Pakistan existed.

Some Pakistanis feel Urdu is a language being forced upon them by the upper classes since many employers will only hire those who speak Urdu. They also feel it is the language of the Muhajir, Muslims who fled India after the two countries separated.

People who oppose Urdu argue that it is not indigenous to the people of Pakistan, while its supporters believe that making Urdu Pakistan's official language gives the nation a common tongue to contribute to its national identity.

Say It in Urdu

hello	assalam-o-assalam
food	khana
help	madad
bread	roti
tea	chai
milk	dood
man	maid
woman	oarat
boy	larhki
girl	larhka
sleep	sona
home	ghan
mosque	masjid
peace	aman

English

English has become the language of business and government in Pakistan since it is spoken around the world and is often the language of international relations. It is spoken by Pakistan's upper classes and by government officials.

Established as the language of bureaucracy in 1956 and again in 1962, English continues to be a second language for most Pakistanis who speak and write it. Many merchants with shops in the bazaars of Pakistan's major cities might also know some English, usually enough to barter with tourists over the cost of their goods or services.

Since 1988, the use of English has declined. Many Pakistanis oppose the adoption and use of English in Pakistan since it was implemented in India when the British occupied the country in the 1800s and early 1900s.

Punjabi

Punjabi is the most commonly spoken language in Pakistan. It is the language of the Punjabi people who make up more than 55 percent of the population, or about

A man peruses the newspapers at a retail stand in Peshawar. Pakistan's literacy rate is 43 percent, meaning approximately 38 million Pakistanis do not have the ability to read or write. Recent efforts to boost Pakistan's overall literacy rate have brought about new agencies devoted to teaching, though the country continues to lag behind most other world nations in these skills.

seventy-nine million people. In India, about 3 percent of the people, those of Punjab descent, also speak Punjabi.

Punjabi has an old literary tradition, with religious and poetic writings dating as far back as AD 1600. However, few people use it as a poetic or literary language today.

Punjabi script uses letters that are influenced by Arabic and Persian, once a great literary language in its own right. Persian is a very old language developed and spoken in Persia (Iran) and is today known as Farsi. Saraiki is a variation of Punjabi spoken by more than fifteen million Pakistanis.

Sindhi

More than twenty million Pakistanis speak Sindhi, a common language in Pakistan's Sindh province. Though Sindhi is an Indo-Aryan language, it is written in a Persian-Arabic alphabet that also resembles the one used to write Urdu. Sindhi writing is different enough from Urdu, however, to make it unique from the Arabic script used to write Urdu. Sometimes these differences in the two scripts make it difficult for the people who read and write Sindhi to read the writing of Urdu.

The Sindhi people have struggled to keep their language since Pakistan became a country. Many of the Muslims who emigrated from India in the late 1940s—the Muhajir—spoke Urdu and did not want to change their language. Most Muhajir were well-educated upper-class people who settled in the growing city of Karachi in southwestern Sindh.

Indigenous Sindhi live mostly in the rural areas of the province, though others are well-educated city dwellers. Violent conflicts have arisen in Karachi in the past fifty years between people who want Sindhi to be the official language and people who want Urdu to remain Pakistan's mother tongue.

Other Languages

Pashtu (or Pathan) is spoken by Pakistanis living in the North-West Frontier Province. In that region, and nearby Baluchistan, more than twelve million people speak Pashtu, another Indo-Aryan language. Pashtu writing is based on Arabic writing. Its earliest texts date back to the 1500s.

Balochi, related more to Persian, is spoken by the Baluchi of Baluchistan in western Pakistan and by people in eastern Iran and parts of Afghanistan. About five million Pakistanis are known to speak Balochi as their first language. People who used this language had no way to write their words until the 1800s when people adjusted Persian and Urdu writing to meet their needs. Today, people write Balochi using a form of Arabic known as *Nasta'liq*.

Smaller groups of people speak more than sixty known languages in Pakistan. People living in the Chitral district of the North-West Frontier Province, for instance, speak a variety of languages. Living among the high peaks of the Hindu Kush, these isolated people developed many languages and dialects, including Kalasha, spoken by an estimated 4,000 members of the Kalash people. Others include Dameli, Kamviri, and Phalura. Kalasha and Dameli are among the six languages of Pakistan considered by linguists to be endangered, or threatened with extinction as people learn more common methods of communication.

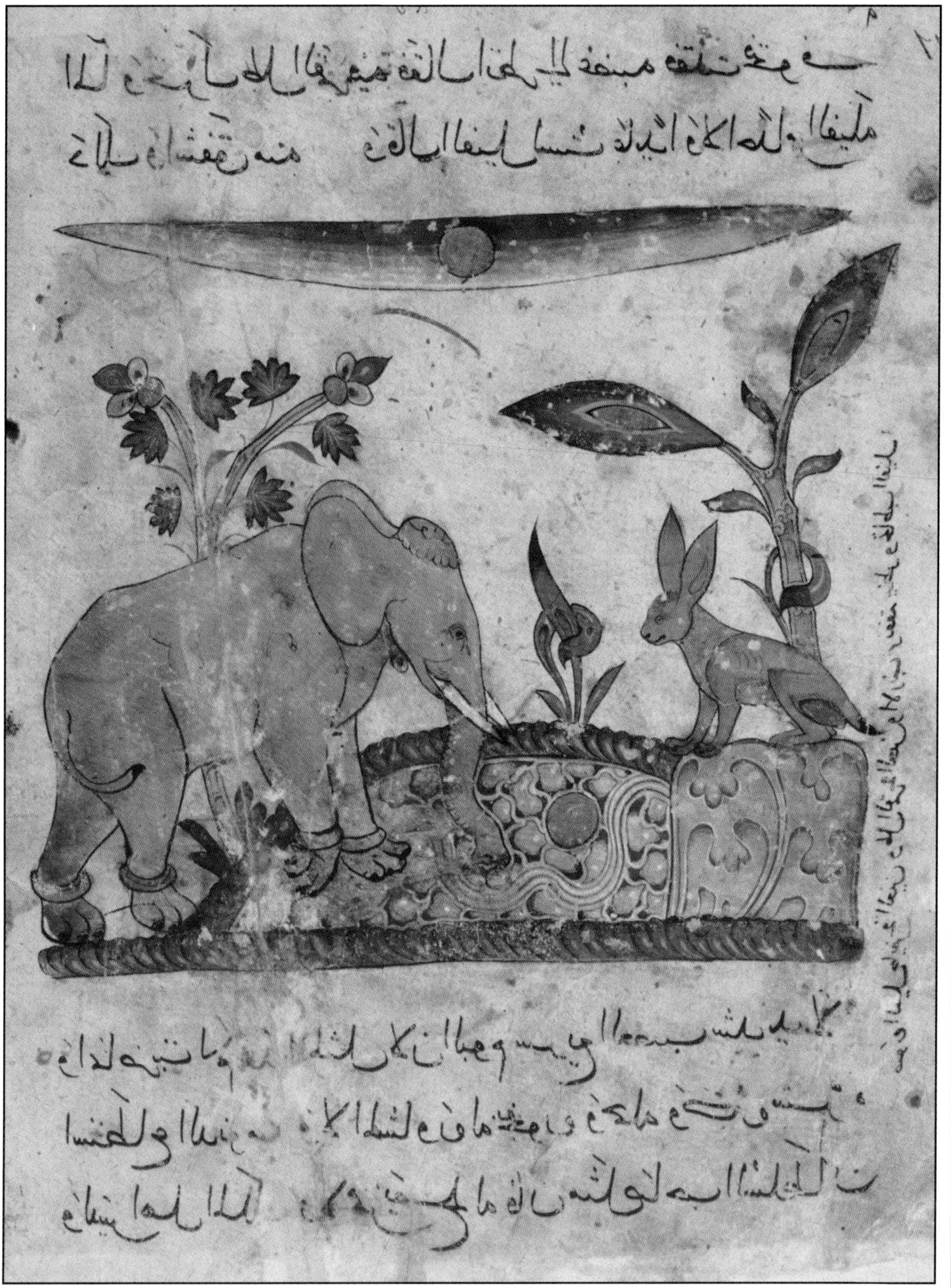

PAKISTANI MYTHS AND LEGENDS

4

M yths and legends are the stories people tell to explain their origin and their culture and to pass on their history. In Pakistan today, people cherish their heroes and stories while creating a national identity for their young country.

When Pakistan became an independent Islamic republic in 1947, the people of what had before been British India had to make a choice. These people could either live in Pakistan, a Muslim country, or live in democratic India, which was destined to be a land where the majority of its residents were Hindus, or followers of Hinduism. For several years before and after independence, millions of people moved across the new border between India and the newly formed Pakistan. Most Muslims chose Pakistan and most Hindus chose India.

People of both nations had shared a long past. Even though much of that past was rooted in a largely Hindu Indian heritage, the Muslims of Pakistan decided to carve a separate path from India. This Islamic nation, where 97 percent of its population is Muslim, chose to honor its Muslim past. To a great extent, they turned away from the legends and stories of the shared past with India's sacred Vedic texts and its Hindu culture.

Pakistan's tribal people, for whom ancestry is a much bigger part of their lives than nationality, have clung to their pasts. The Baluchi people of southwestern and

This fourteenth-century Arabic book illumination *(left)* is titled the "The Elephant and the Hare." A bronze statue of the Hindu god Siva *(above)* dates from the sixth century BC. Siva's name literally means "auspicious." Often portrayed as a king, yogi, or ascetic in Hindu art and mythology, he is known as the god that destroys. His destructive powers ultimately lead to good, however, since he removes impurity for the sake of liberation. His importance earns him the place as the third member of the Hindu Trinity.

This young child from the Rabari tribe in the border town of Nagarparkar in the Tharparkar desert region of Pakistan's Sindh province is wearing a necklace made of old clothing and buttons. Known in Pakistan as a *taveez*, it is believed that the necklace will protect him from evil spirits. Although not a Muslim practice, it contains verses of the Koran inscribed on the buttons.

western Pakistan and the Pushtun of northwestern Pakistan still tell the stories of their great ancestral heroes. Sindh and Punjabi people still tell the tales told by their grandparents.

Islam

Muslims revere Muhammad, the prophet who began their religion in AD 610. They do not, however, regard him as more than human. He is not a god. Fanciful stories told of Muhammad would be considered heresy, or false teaching, to a faithful Muslim.

Some of the symbols of the Prophet's life, however, are common in Pakistan's art. For instance, the horse that carried Muhammad to heaven, Al-Buraq, often pictured with wings and a human head, is frequently painted on murals and Pakistan's famous painted delivery trucks.

The Koran records the messages Muhammad received throughout his life from Allah through the help of the archangel Gabriel. People who believed in the mythologies popular during Muhammad's life (AD 570–632) were considered unbelievers. In the Islamic religion, only God created this world and it is He who watches over humanity. Unlike Hinduism, there are no other gods about whom to create legends. There is no pantheon of greater and lesser gods as in Greek, Roman, or Norse mythology.

Islamic Pirs

Many of the Muslims of Pakistan honor the memory of the *pirs*, or Sufi teachers of Islam. (Sufism is considered by some Muslims to be a mystical sect of Islam, though it is not defined in Pakistan as a sect in the same way that Muslims can be defined by either the Sunni or Shiite sects.) These Sufis were wise men who traveled the land, without wealth or home, to share the teachings of Allah. These men were

Islamic mystics who shared their wisdom, teachings, and contemplations of Allah with all people, particularly the poor and the lowly. Pirs are said to have special abilities to cure illnesses, foretell the future, and perform miracles.

People honor these men by visiting their tombs on the anniversary of their deaths. Artists paint posters of the more popular pirs. People display copies of these posters in their homes and outside of the pirs' tombs and shrines. A shrine to Syed Abdul Latif Shah, a seventeenth-century Sufi mystic, stands in the center of Nurpur, a village in Punjab. On the anniversary of Hazrat Mehr Ali Shah's death, more than one million pilgrims visit his shrine in the village of Golra Sharif near the city of Islamabad.

Onlookers crowd around a woman whom they believe is possessed by the spirits inside the mausoleum of Sheikh Osman of Marwand in the town of Sehwan Sharif. Osman belonged to the Qalandar denomination of Persian Sufis, who clothed themselves in coarse woolen dresses tightened by bark girdles. These people practiced austerity and contemplation as they transported themselves into ecstasy. Osman is regarded as a saint with devotees among both Muslims and Hindus.

Tribal Legends and Folktales

The Baluchi people of southwestern Pakistan revere their tribal heroes. Their epic poems have passed on orally the exploits of their ancestors for generations. The stories of Mir

The Rat Who Made One Bargain Too Many

A West Pakistani folktale from *Toontoony Pie*, retold by the author

One day, a clever rat picked up a stick he found in the middle of the road. Soon he met a father struggling to build a fire to warm his children. "The wood is too wet," said the man. "Here, take this dry stick," said the rat. Saying thank you, the man gave the rat a bit of bread dough. The rat soon came upon two boys crying in the yard of a potter. "What is the matter?" asked the rat. "Our parents are late coming home and we are hungry," said the boys. "Then bake this dough," said the rat. With thanks, the boys gave the rat a clay pot. The rat then came to a man milking a buffalo, squirting the milk into a dirty shoe. "It would be better to put that milk in a clean pail," said the rat. "Yes it would be," said the man, "if I had a pail." The rat gave the man the clay pot. The man finished milking the buffalo and offered the rat some milk. "A drink for a nice clean pot?" exclaimed the rat. "I deserve more. Give me your buffalo." Laughing, the man tied the buffalo's rope around the rat's neck. The rat continued walking, but the rope only tightened. He turned to see his buffalo grazing by the roadside. "I suppose this buffalo knows better than I where the best food is," said the rat. For the rest of the day, the rat scurried after the grazing buffalo. When the beast came to rest by a stream, the rat dropped to the ground exhausted. Soon he heard people talking and looked up to find a wedding procession coming near. Four men carried a bride on a curtained chaise. They complained of the heavy load and of their hunger. The rat, seeing a chance for a bargain, said, "Cook this fine buffalo." The men accepted. They offered some of the roasted meat to the rat. "A bite of dinner for that great buffalo? Give me the bride you carry," the rat demanded. The frightened men ran away. The rat opened the curtains and saw a beautiful woman. Frightened by her isolation in the woods, the bride followed the rat home and accepted his offer of two peas for dinner. The next day, the rat found some luscious plums and gave them to the bride who took them to town to sell. There, she came across the queen, her mother, who had been searching for the bride. When the queen and the bride turned toward the palace, the rat shouted at the queen, "I demand my bride!" The queen looked down at him and said, "Of course. We were preparing a warm chamber for you." Excited by his good fortune, the rat followed the queen into the palace. "Here we are," said the queen, and she opened the door to a stove in which burned a large fire. The eager rat jumped into the "warm chamber" and the queen slammed the door behind him. "A trick!" shouted the rat. "What a bad bargain. I shall never make another bargain in my life." Upon hearing the rat's vow, the queen finally opened the door.

The Shrine of Shams Tabriz, made entirely of sky-blue engravings with glazed brick, is located in the city of Multan in Pakistan. Shams Tabriz was the spiritual master of Rumi, founder of the Mevlevi Sufi order, a mystical sect of Islam, and great mystic poet of Persia. According to legend, Shams Tabriz was flayed alive and he wandered for four days with his skin in his hand.

Chakur, a sixteenth-century tribal chief, still fill the tents of these seminomadic people. Chakur was also a warrior of the Rind people who struggled against Gwaharam, a warrior for the Lashari. The leaders taunt each other in battle and in words in a famous epic poem known as *Chakur and Gwaharam*. After the development of a Baluchi script in the nineteenth century, Baluchi artists and storytellers began sharing the stories that are uniquely their own.

Folktales also thrive in Punjab. The heroes of these stories are very often animals. Similar to ancient Indian folktales, jackals appear in many Pakistani stories as wise tricksters. Monkeys, tigers, and birds sometimes learn the lessons of wisdom and kindness.

Human tales occasionally focus on the heartbreak of lovers. The story of Hir and Ranjha, a very old Punjabi tale, explains efforts of star-crossed lovers who marry and live in peace only to be continually thwarted by their families.

Sindh legends frequently involve stories of conflict between Muslims and Hindus. The close relationship between the Sindh people of Pakistan and their Indian Hindu neighbors has remained a part of their legends despite the separation of their land between two countries. Some Sindh stories even feature Hindu gods of their neighbors.

PAKISTANI FESTIVALS AND CEREMONIES OF ANTIQUITY AND TODAY

5

Although Pakistan's festivals and ceremonies are largely religious, there are several that celebrate the country's more secular sense of nationalism. In rural areas, other common celebrations revolve around changing seasons, such as the final weeks of the harvest. From the birth ceremonies and holy feasts of Islam, to the celebrations of the nation's founding father, the people of Pakistan frequently gather to play music, to pray, and even to wrestle. Fireworks and special foods help to make these events even more spectacular.

National Festivals

Many Pakistanis living today experienced the creation of their country. People who were born after 1947 have stories to remind them of the hardship, the pain, and finally the rejoicing that followed partition. As millions of people fled their homes across the new border, ethnic violence killed more than 250,000 people. Between twelve and twenty-five million people crossed the new border seeking a safe home. Pakistanis now celebrate their nation's birth with four major holidays.

Special ceremonies in the provincial capitals—Karachi, Quetta, Peshawar, and Lahore—as well as in Islamabad, honor Pakistan Day on March 23. This holiday

Pakistani soldiers *(left)* hang a large banner of Muhammad Ali Jinnah as part of the celebrations for Pakistan Day, which is celebrated on March 23. This holiday commemorates the date that Pakistan declared itself an Islamic republic, signing its constitution on March 23, 1956. Until that time, Pakistan had been operating under a working constitution put in place by England's Indian Independence Act of 1947. A vendor *(above)* sells the traditional foods of Ramadan, the ninth month of the Muslim calendar. Throughout Ramadan, Muslims fast during daylight and eat a small meal after sunset. Pakistanis are known for their love of food and normally break their fast by sharing a variety of foods with other Muslims.

Troops from the Frontier Constabulary, a wing of the national army, march during Pakistan Day in Islamabad. In creating the 1956 constitution, which officially recognized Pakistan as an Islamic republic, the government leaders sought to create an independent Islamic nation. In accordance with the new constitution, the Muslim president was required to establish an organization for Islamic research to serve its Muslim citizens.

commemorates the 1956 constitutional resolution that proclaimed Pakistan an Islamic republic. In 2002, the celebrations were more subdued, as thousands of Pakistani soldiers stationed on its eastern border continued the conflict with India over Jammu and Kashmir, a territory claimed by both nations since 1947.

Flag raising, moments of silence, and political rallies celebrate Independence Day—the founding of Pakistan—on August 14–15. The playing of the national anthem honors the day Pakistan signed the declaration of independence from Great Britain and separation from India. Everyone has a chance to participate in Independence Day celebrations since schools and government agencies are closed.

Both Muhammad Ali Jinnah's birthday, December 25, and the anniversary of his death, September 11, give Pakistanis reason to celebrate. Jinnah, known as the *Quaid-e-Azam*, or founder of the country, fought hard in the 1930s and 1940s to create a separate Muslim nation. Both days are considered public holidays. People pay their respects with fireworks, select cuisine, and visits to sites important in his life, such as his tomb in Karachi.

September 6 marks Defense of Pakistan Day, or the commemoration of the 1965 Indo-Pakistani War, followed by the November 9 celebration of Pakistan's honorable national poet Allama Muhammad Iqbal.

Religious Festivals

The biggest religious celebration in all of Pakistan is Eid-ul-Fiter (also known as Chhoti Eid), the celebration that marks the end of Ramadan, the ritualistic month of fasting for Muslims. This is the biggest feast of the Islamic faith, typically celebrated by a pilgrimage to the largest mosques. Families gather for special prayer services and huge feasts that begin after sundown beginning the last day of Ramadan. Adults and children greet one another exclaiming, "Eid mubarak," or "an auspicious Eid to you." They also wear their best clothing, which is often embellished with regional trimmings. Camels are adorned with brightly colored fabrics.

The exact date of Eid-ul-Fiter moves with the lunar calendar used to determine the dates of Islamic events. To Westerners, this religious celebration is similar to Christmas since children normally receive gifts, employees receive bonuses, and schools and businesses are closed for several days. It is also customary during Eid-ul-Fiter

This illustration depicts the Feast of the Sacrifice (Eid-ul-Adha) in Pakistan. The Feast of the Sacrifice is an important occasion in the Muslim calendar and is celebrated by the slaughter of goats. It commemorates Abraham's willingness to sacrifice his son in the name of Allah. Muslims believe that the spirit of sacrifice demonstrates love for Allah over self-love.

The butchers in this photograph are cleaning the carcass of a goat that was sacrificed during the Feast of the Sacrifice in Karachi, Pakistan. Pakistanis prefer meat to vegetables, especially during social occasions. Meat is killed according to the *halal* process of slaughtering and draining the animal's blood. Butchers then carefully remove all the fat in order to preserve the freshness of the meat for a longer period.

to give money and food to the poorest people of the community.

Ten weeks after Eid-ul-Fiter, Muslims in Pakistan celebrate Eid-ul-Adha (also known as Bari Eid), or the Feast of the Sacrifice, which commemorates Abraham's willingness to sacrifice his son Isaac in the name of Allah. Abraham is an Islamic prophet.

The slaughtering of a male goat, sheep, or calf marks this four-day celebration. Whoever does the actual killing, whether a family member or a butcher, will say the word *Bismillah*, which translates as "in the name of Allah." Normally, this sacrificial animal will be divided into three portions allowing enough meat for the immediate family, relatives, and the poor, who receive the largest and last portion.

Another important religious celebration in Pakistan is the anniversary of the death of various caliphs, or spiritual leaders of Islam. The celebration commemorating Ali Hussein (also known as Ali al-Husayn), occurs on the tenth day of Muharram, the first month in the Muslim calendar. Hussein was the third caliph of the Shiites and

Pakistani Muslims pray before breaking their first fast of the Islamic holy month, Ramadan, at the shrine of Data Ganj Bakhsh in Lahore. Every day thousands of Muslims make devotions at the tomb. Data Ganj Bakhsh, also known as the Bestower of Favors, is the patron saint of Lahore.

the son of Fatimah, the daughter of Muhammad. He was massacred during the Battle of Karbala more than 1,300 years ago when Islam split into the sects of Sunni and Shiite, and is known as the Prince of Martyrs.

The most important day in this festival for Muslims occurs on the tenth day, which is known as Ashura. Muslims celebrate Ashura by fasting, being charitable, visiting the sick and dying, and praying. Grand public processions are held across Pakistan in celebration of this festival, which begins the next year. For Muslims, this is a time of selflessness, patience, and sacrifice. While Sunni Muslims celebrate Hussein's death by shutting down public entertainment for ten days, devout Shiite Muslims perform acts of self-flagellation that reenact Hussein's suffering. Crying out in the name of the martyr, these Shiites have their backs beaten with whips and chains until they bleed.

Finally, all Pakistanis gather at fairs to celebrate the *urs*, or death anniversaries, of famous holy men. Pakistanis travel to the saints' tombs to pay homage to the teachings of these religious men. One of the sites of the three-day festival is the Mausoleum of Sheikh Osman, known as Shah Lal Baz Qalandar, located in Sindh. Osman's death is often honored by the enactment of marriage ceremonies that represent the saint's communion with Allah. Musicians, singers, and dancers gather among the people to entertain. Food stalls open, and people join together to celebrate these local heroes.

Cultural Festivals

Although religion is a very important part of the culture of Pakistan, cultural traditions are also a cause to celebrate. Many ethnic groups in Pakistan also hold specific gatherings.

Pakistanis in Lahore celebrate spring with a kite-flying festival called Basant. Kite flying became associated with spring sometime in the Middle Ages. However, it is not a subdued pastime in Pakistan. Opponents compete in the *pecha*, or kite fight, with string dipped in powdered glass to cut their rivals' kites down from the sky.

One of the most popular festivals in Pakistan occurs annually in the city of Lahore. Called the Basant festival, this celebration is a day when Pakistanis of all ages get together to fly kites for pleasure and competition. Interesting to Westerners is that the kite strings in Pakistan are often coated with ground glass capable of cutting the strings of other kites that cross its path. As soon as one kite downs another and drops it, crowds of Pakistanis roar with delight. This colorful display takes place in March and marks the start of spring.

Arts and crafts fairs—called *melas*—also attract people to regional centers, as do sporting events. These melas often feature circus-type performances, merry-go-rounds and other amusements, as well as ritual dancing. The national folk festival *Lok Virsa*, also known as *Lok Mela*, attracts musicians and artisans from around the world. Artists perform in pavilions and sell their handicrafts. This five-day festival gives Pakistanis, as well as international travelers, the opportunity to share the cultural beauty of this land.

Agriculture is often celebrated in Baluchistan, where horse and cattle shows abound. Lahore in Punjab also hosts the annual national horse and cattle show for five days every November.

The small tribal community of the Kalash, who live among the rugged mountains of northern Pakistan, celebrates the annual walnut and grape harvest with the *Phool* festival in September, welcomes winter with *Chowmas* (the first snowfall festival in October), and welcomes spring with *Joshi* in May.

Family Celebrations

Perhaps the most festive celebrations in all of Pakistan are weddings. These celebrations often last

A groom dressed in traditional Sindhi wedding dress rides to his bride's home in a marriage procession called a *baraat*. When he reaches the house, her family welcomes him with garlands. The bride's sisters and brothers then ask him to come inside. He calls to his mother to lead the way, and she, in turn, asks the married women of the baraat to accompany them.

for three days. The bride wears a colorful gown and glitters with jewelry decorating her head, arms, ears, and nose. On the first day before the ceremony, the bride and groom hold a party where they paint designs on their hands with henna. Guests celebrate with a traditional feast, music, and songs. On the second day, the bride's family hosts a huge celebration where the actual ceremonies are performed. On the third day, the groom's family invites friends to continue the festivities.

Special occasions such as the birth of a child are also cause to celebrate—especially the arrival of a son. In Baluchistan, the arrival of a boy is cause for music, dancing, and baking and eating sweets.

In traditional Sindh villages, families commemorate births with a head-shaving ritual when their children are three to four weeks old. They sacrifice goats—one for a girl and two for a boy—and feast on the meat. Lastly, they bury the goat's bones with the baby's hair to bring good fortune.

A Muslim couple wearing traditional dress is married in Karachi. Before a Pakistani wedding takes place, there are days of feasting, exchanging presents, displaying gifts, and the important Mehndi ceremony, which is the joining of the two families. For that ceremony, the bride wears a decorative red scarf and dress, and her hands and feet are decorated with henna designs and jewels. The groom wears a ring of flowers around his neck. Afterward, an elaborate reception is held where the men and women dine separately.

THE RELIGIONS OF PAKISTAN THROUGHOUT ITS HISTORY

6

N early all Pakistanis, more than 140 million people, are Muslim. The Islamic Republic of Pakistan exists because of the desire of Muslims to have a separate Islamic state from India, which is largely home to Hindus. When Great Britain ruled India in the late 1800s and early 1900s, the Muslims living there represented a minority group. Muslims felt discriminated against by the Indian Hindu majority. They wanted certain Indian provinces to be ruled by Muslims so they could follow the laws of Islam instead of the laws of the state.

In the early 1900s, Muslim leaders struggled to convince British rulers to make some of the northern provinces Muslim ruled, during which time Great Britain decided to completely renounce its rule of India. In negotiating the transfer of its power, Great Britain eventually agreed that this huge peninsula of south Asia should be divided into two countries, India and Pakistan, a separation that finally came in 1947.

Millions of Muslims then living in India fled to the newly partitioned Pakistan, while millions of Hindus living in the territory that became Pakistan fled to India. Both Muslims and Hindus feared attacks from each other as ethnic hatred fueled by discrimination increased.

But even though India was predominantly Hindu, the lands that both India and Pakistan once shared have, over the centuries, been the home of many religions

This Muslim man *(left)* sits on a rock by a river and the Himalaya Mountains in the town of Gilgit in northern Pakistan. Badshahi Mosque *(above)*, which literally means "king's mosque," is also known as the Imperial Mosque of Aurangzeb Alamgir. A marble inscription dates the mosque's construction to AD 1673. It reads, "For Aurangzeb by Fidai Khan." Its courtyard is the largest in the world, receiving up to 100,000 people for prayer during open-air congregational meetings in the shadow of the four striking minarets.

This ancient Hindu temple lies outside of the village of Gori. Legends state that a rich Hindu merchant established the foundation around the middle of the sixteenth century. Frescoes in the main dome depict princesses in royal coaches, equestrian processions, and women in flowing robes tending to household chores. The pillared interior is marble and the Prasanth icon, believed to be studded with one large diamond between its eyes and two smaller ones on its breasts, was removed from the temple in 1716 and since lost.

including Zoroastrianism, Hinduism, Buddhism, Islam, Judaism, and finally, Christianity. Three of today's major religions had important roles to play in Pakistan's history, however, beginning with Hinduism.

Hinduism

India was and is the center of the ancient Hindu religion, which originated more than 3,500 years ago. Much of the area in which Hinduism originated is now Pakistan. The word "Hindu" is derived from *sindhu,* the Sanskrit word for "river." The earliest form of Hinduism was practiced during the Vedic period and was brought into the Indus River valley by Aryan invaders from central Asia. These warrior people had strong beliefs in their gods. By 900 BC, they pushed their empire east to the Ganges River and carried with them beliefs in a pantheon of gods who influenced all aspects of human life.

The heart of the Hindu religion is the Vedas, sacred literature composed during the Vedic period. Written in Sanskrit, the original hymns were probably written between 1300 and 1000 BC. The Vedas were first recited orally and later written, reaching their present form in about AD 200.

Hindus believe in a wide variety of gods, in reincarnation, and in the caste system, which stems from the rule of the Aryans, when, as victors, they discriminated against India's indigenous population.

Hinduism was well established before Islam arrived in the eighth century AD. For centuries, worshipers of both religions peacefully coexisted. During the reign of various emperors, religious tolerance between Muslims and Hindus decreased, and people often became violent. During this process, imagery, idols, and places of worship including temples and mosques were destroyed.

Many years later, during the British occupation of India, Hindus, often favored by the British, gained positions in society and were often better educated than Muslims. This separation of power contributed to civil unrest in India. Violence spread rapidly, and, at the time that the subcontinent was partitioned, Muslims living within India fled across the new border to Pakistan. Hindus living in what had become Pakistan returned to India. Many people—regardless of their beliefs—had become refugees who gave up their homelands after partition.

Buddhism

In northeastern India, near the border of Nepal, Siddhartha Gautama was born into a wealthy royal family in 563 BC. At the time of his early life, Hinduism was

This stone relief from the second century BC shows monks, princes, and bodhisattvas worshiping Buddha. Asoka, emperor of the Mauryan Empire, brought Buddhism to Pakistan and much of Asia as an act of remorse for the suffering caused by his conquests.

This miniature Mughal painting portrays Babur the Great. Babur, a compassionate ruler, brought Islam to India through his conquests of the country. He would not allow his troops to harm or plunder innocent people and was highly cultured, writing poetry as well as his memoirs, known as the *Baburnama*, in both Persian and Turkish.

India's religion, then practiced mostly by Brahmin priests who controlled the religious process. As a boy, Siddhartha was instructed in Hindu beliefs and educated by the Vedas.

Because he was born into royalty and slated to one day become king, Siddhartha's father sheltered him from the horrors of life, such as sickness and death. From a young age, musicians and dancers entertained the prince, and servants tended to his every whim. As Siddhartha grew, his father arranged for his marriage, and soon Siddhartha fathered his own son. Although he was fortunate and successful, the prince was discontented.

One day, despite his father's efforts, the legend tell us that Siddhartha came across an elderly man suffering from old age. At this discovery, he traveled farther and found another man whose life had been ravaged by a debilitating illness. Finally, Siddhartha was confronted with death. The once innocent prince had witnessed a funeral procession and had seen a corpse for the first time. Finally, on his fourth journey, as the legend recounts, Siddhartha met a wandering monk. This man, despite his own suffering, appeared to be perfectly at peace with the world and its horrors. Siddhartha now believed that he, too, needed to understand sickness and death.

On his twenty-ninth birthday, Siddhartha renounced his material possessions and left his family. He set out with a servant and his horse to make his own way in the world. After traveling many miles, Siddhartha sent his servant and horse away. He cut his long black hair and exchanged his silk clothing for cotton cloth. Siddhartha was now a wandering monk on a spiritual quest.

Pushing the limits of his physical body, Siddhartha, now known as Sakyamuni, pursued a higher spiritual enlightenment through meditation and decreased desire. His goal was to become selfless. Eventually, after years of meditation and fasting, he was now enlightened and known as the Buddha. From the age of thirty-five, the Buddha spent his days as a compassionate teacher advising others of what he had learned. He now had followers who would spread Buddhism after his death. The monks who continued his teachings spread the Four Noble Truths of suffering, ignorance, knowledge, and right living.

Unlike Hinduism, Buddhism was open to all people regardless of their gender or caste. Even the "untouchables," the lowest members of India's caste system, a strict social structure that divided the population into various classes, could become Buddhists.

Buddhism arrived in the land of the Indus River valley in the third century BC. Missionaries sent there by Buddhist leaders spread its philosophies, which denied many of the Hindu teachings, particularly those of the caste system. The meditative spirituality of Buddhism influenced the people of Taxila, a prominent city on the Silk Road, an ancient trading route that linked Europe to China. The influence of Buddhism turned a young warrior ruler, Asoka, to more peaceful ways. Asoka's conversion led him to order that Buddhist messages be written on pillars scattered across the land. Two survive to this day.

Taxila was the capital of the Gandharan region of northern Pakistan. For more than 500 years, the artists of the area were influenced by the styles of conquering Greeks and Persians, therefore, sculptural representations of Buddha from Gandhara are known for their distinctly European features.

Although not currently practiced in Pakistan, Buddhism thrived in much of India until the arrival

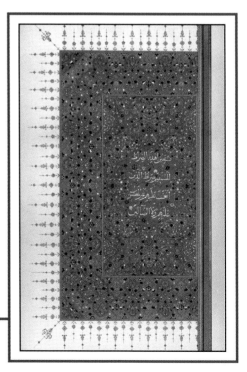

The image of the Koran pictured here shows the opening page of its first *sura*, or chapter. The Koran is the Muslim holy book, consisting of 114 suras, and is believed to be the written word of Muhammad. Pakistan's current administration is moving toward a more Islamic-controlled government. A law was passed in 1998 that gave the federal government the power to impose laws based on the Koran.

of Muslims in the eighth century AD. Today, Buddhist art in Pakistan remains a great treasure of its people.

Islam

In AD 711, Muhammad bin Qasim, a Persian general, landed on the shores of Sindh with 6,000 Syrian soldiers. His mission was to conquer Sindh and bring Islam into India.

The Islamic faith began in AD 610 when Muhammad, a forty-year-old merchant from Mecca, began hearing the word of Allah during times of meditation in caves near that city. For fifteen years, he had sought understanding of the pagan world in which he lived. During one night of contemplation in a cave on Mount Hira, an angel appeared to Muhammad and commanded him to proclaim Allah's word. Over the next twenty-three years, Muhammad had many visits by this angel during these hours of contemplation. He heard proclaimed to him the holy words that would become the Koran. During those years of proclamation, Muhammad fled Mecca for Medina, taking with him the first Muslims. Muhammad died in AD 632 as the spiritual leader and ruler of Medina.

During his lifetime, Muhammad and his followers memorized and recited the Koran. Scholars believe that they may have written most of the verses on loose pieces of parchment as aids to their memory. After Muhammad's death, his successor as leader of Islam, Abu Bakr, ordered the proclamations written and preserved. The Koran became Islam's holy book.

Pakistani Muslims offer prayer to victims of the terrorist attacks of September 11, 2001. Muslims in Pakistan make up 97 percent of the population. The Islamic view of society and the goal of all Muslims is "Allah's rule on earth." Although Pakistan's constitution defines the country as an Islamic nation, it does guarantee freedom of religion.

Islam spread quickly across the Middle East and also into Asia. By the time Muhammad bin Qasim arrived in Sindh, Islam was less than a century old. During the next 800 years, Islam flourished on the subcontinent, coexisting with other religions. In 1526, Babur, the first of the great Mughal rulers, moved his army from Kabul (Afghanistan) into India. By 1529, he had established an Islamic empire across all of India; this empire survived until the 1800s.

Since partition, Islam has been a powerful force, and its principles have helped to form its government. As an Islamic republic, religion plays a significant role in how leaders govern Pakistan. Many of the laws and principles of international relations are determined by Islamic law and theology.

Muslims believe that the Koran is the revealed word of Allah, and revere Muhammad for bringing that word to them. Today, there are about seventy various sects, or divisions, of Islam in Pakistan, some of which follow these tenets. The Five Pillars of Islam present the principles that regulate a Muslim's life.

Today, Islam is divided into two major sects: Sunni and Shiite. They have their origins in the years following Muhammad's death and differ in which of the *hadiths*, or teachings of the prophets, they believe are authentic. In Pakistan, 77 percent of the people are Sunni Muslims and 20 percent are Shiites.

People of different ethnic groups in Pakistan bring their ancestral traditions to Islam and may interpret the teachings of past leaders differently. Some Baluchi, for instance, belong to another sect of Islam known as Zakri. They are followers of a fifteenth-century Muslim who interpreted the teachings of the Koran and Muhammad differently than do the Sunni or Shiite Muslims. Most Muslims do not regard Zakri as true believers of Islam, though the Zakri do see themselves as Muslims. Zakri do not follow the Five Pillars of Islam or follow the concept of a religion-based government.

Some Baluchi and many Sindhi from southeastern Pakistan are passionate followers of *pirs*. These Sufi teachers, believed to hear the direct word of Allah, have offered their influence since their belief strongly influenced the Baluchi and Sindhi people.

Other Religions

Only 3 percent of the people in Pakistan follow the teachings of other religions, including Sikhism and Buddhism. These groups, however, deserve some attention, especially since followers of these minority religions report that they frequently face discrimination.

The Five Pillars of Islam

The Muslims of Pakistan vary in their expressions of their religion from other Muslims. Their daily lives are influenced, to varying degrees, by the following:

The first pillar is known in Arabic as *shahada*, which means bearing witness to Allah, the one God, and to Muhammad as his messenger. The second pillar is called *salat*, which means performing the ritual prayers of Islam, generally at the prescribed times of day. Muhammad was directed to tell Muslims to pray five times each day: at dawn, at midday, during the late afternoon, at sunset, and during the night. *Zakat* is the third pillar of Islam and means giving alms, or charity. Through the act of sharing their surplus in life, Muslims seek to cleanse themselves from the influences of greed and selfishness. Giving charity is seen as a religious requirement, but in Pakistan where Islamic law is part of its national law, governments have required people to pay *zakat* in the form of a tax. The fourth pillar of Islam is known as *sawm*, the ritual fast during the month of Ramadan. During Ramadan, Muslims do not eat or drink from sunrise to sunset. The fifth and final pillar is *hajj*, the pilgrimage to Mecca. Each Muslim is obliged to visit the holy city of Mecca in Saudi Arabia, the birthplace of Muhammad, at least once in his or her lifetime, if he or she is physically and financially able.

Sikhism began in the early 1500s in the Punjab area of northern India, parts of which are now in both Pakistan and India. This monotheistic religion combines aspects of Hinduism and Islam. Sikhs accept the role of meditation in religion, but also

A Sikh priest recites from the Sikh sacred book (Granth Sahib) during a religious celebration in Punjab, India. Guru Nanak, founder of the Sikh religion, was born near Lahore, Pakistan, in 1469. After the separation of Pakistan from India, many Sikhs migrated to India. Pakistan's Sikh shrines are maintained by the government and visited annually during Sikh festivals.

believe in the Hindu concepts of reincarnation and *karma*—the force that is the sum of a person's actions—in this life and in other lives. A border separates Pakistani Sikhs from the religion's most holy temple in Amristar, India. Many feel they deserve their own homeland and argue for reuniting the parts of historical Punjab into one Sikh homeland, or independent country.

About 1 percent of Pakistanis are Christians. They believe that Jesus Christ is the son of God and follow his teachings. Christianity seems to have arrived in the northwestern region of India from many routes. Some people believe Thomas, one of Jesus' twelve disciples, traveled to India after Jesus' crucifixion. Europeans in the 1200s would have brought the teachings of Jesus as they traveled along the Silk Road to reach China. British Christians came to the land with the traders and military troops of the British Empire from the 1600s to the formation of Pakistan in 1947.

A Hindu priest is outside his temple in a rural area near Omekot in the Sindh province. Hindu temples have been subject to periodic violence at the hands of the Muslim majority population, mainly as a result of issues between Hindus and Muslims in India. In Pakistan, Hindus are the religious minority, with the Hindu population dropping from 23 percent in 1947, to less than 3 percent in 2003.

THE ART AND ARCHITECTURE OF PAKISTAN

7

The buildings and artwork of the civilizations that preceded today's Islamic Republic of Pakistan are a part of its everyday life. Craftspeople creating jewelry in the bazaars of Lahore or Karachi still use designs and techniques similar to those used by their ancient ancestors.

Because Islam has been a part of this land since the eighth century, the religion has a very strong influence on modern painting, sculpture, and architecture. Seventeenth-century mosques such as the Badshahi in Lahore and Jamia Masjid—the mosque of Shah Jahan—in the Sindh province represent some of the most striking architecture of the land.

More than twenty-five museums in Pakistan preserve the cultural remains of these civilizations while sharing with the public the treasures being created by modern artists. Art galleries also abound in cities such as Karachi and Lahore.

Gandharan Art

The first true artistic period in the region now known as Pakistan occurred within the ancient kingdom of Gandhara. This area thrived around 200 BC in the temperate foothills of the Koshkoram Mountains in north central Pakistan. One of its capital cities, Taxila, was an important cultural and trading center, the heart of a growing

A woman's position in Pakistani society determines the clothing she prefers. While many upper-class women wear Western-styled clothing such as sleeveless shirts and jeans, many women of the middle and lower classes, such as this woman *(left)*, wear the traditional clothing called a *shalwar kaameez* and a head scarf. The Badshahi Mosque *(above)* was built during the Mughal occupation of the area of present-day Pakistan. Mughal architecture is revered for its blend of grace, strength, and harmony.

A stone sculpture of the Fasting Buddha dates from the second or third century AD. It stands as the greatest masterpiece of the Buddhist Gandharan civilization, which was located in northwest Pakistan. Themes of the Buddha fasting were popular in art produced in Gandhara. This sculpture was one of the first to blend Hellenistic and Indian styles with art that is Roman in form and Buddhist in motif.

Buddhist nation. It stood at the crossroads of the ancient routes and would become a business center on the Silk Road. Today Taxila is an important archaeological site, actually made up of three cities built during changing empires, and located 45 miles (72 kilometers) northwest of Islamabad, Pakistan's capital city.

Gandharan art comes from the Indo-Greek period of India's history. In art and architecture, it captures the essence of both the Greek Hellenistic culture and the Buddhist religion that dominated life in this kingdom. The Greek influence arrived with the conquering armies of Alexander the Great, who reached the city in 326 BC. The Greeks who remained after the army left retained their culture, and around 100 BC, helped to build a new Taxila in the style of Athens.

Buildings and monuments, as well as tombs and statues, were decorated with intricate relief sculptures, much of it telling stories of Buddha's life. Hundreds of *stupas*—dome-shaped Buddhist shrines—were built during this period. Sculptures show everyday people in daily activities. Gandharan sculptors, the main artists of this period, used local stone and sometimes plaster to create their art. Gandharan art is a highly treasured style, where statues of Buddha are sculpted to appear as if he is robed in layers of draping fabric. One of the most famous Gandharan sculptures is known as the Fasting Buddha. Much work from this period is now located in museums in Lahore, Peshawar, and Karachi.

Mughal Empire

The Mughal Empire dominated culture in south Asia for more than 300 years. From 1526 to 1857, the land that is now Pakistan was the northwestern portion of that empire. Fabulous art and architecture are highlights of the Mughal rulers. They built some of the grandest and most colorful buildings in the world, including the Taj Mahal in Agra, India, built in the early 1600s by Mughal emperor Shah Jahan as his wife's tomb. He was entombed there, also, when he died in 1666.

In Pakistan, the Mughal emperors left lasting monuments across the region, from the gates of Peshawar to the huge fort of Lahore, which was a sixteenth-century provincial capital during the height of the empire. Magnificent gardens dominated most Mughal cities such as Sheikhupura and Hiran Minar, which contained a huge hunting complex and was created by the son of Akbar during the reign of Shah Jahan.

Jehangir's Mausoleum was built in 1637 near Lahore, Pakistan, and holds the body of the fourth Mughal emperor Jehangir. Literature and the arts flourished during his reign as well as the integration of Islamic and Indian architecture. Jehangir's mausoleum stands as one of the greatest Mughal structures, made from red sandstone and marble, and with perfect geometrical symmetry. Jehangir's marble grave is elaborately inlaid with floral designs, the ninety-nine attributes of Allah on its sides, and a verse from the Koran on its top.

This miniature painting from the *Baburnama* was completed in 1530. Early Mughal rulers in India brought with them a love and demand for illustrated books and manuscripts. Founder of the Mughal Empire, Babur, and his son Humayun both shared a passion for literature and the arts. However, it was Humayun's son, Akbar the Great, who further cultivated the arts by establishing a workshop of artists from all over India to represent the various indigenous styles.

As a capital city, Lahore once contained six lavish gardens, including the gardens of Lahore's fort. These gardens contained the original Shish Mahal, or Hall of Mirrors—a series of underground caves and tunnels, parade grounds, and assembly spaces. The Mughal emperors built extensive gardens to rival the lush mountains of Kashmir, with water for irrigation that was diverted through canals from the rivers of Punjab. In the Shalimar Gardens, lines of fountains decorate huge sheets of shimmering water. Newer gardens now compliment this old Mughal paradise.

Miniature Painting

At roughly the same time as the Mughals, a style of painting known as the Rajput school from the Punjab area flourished. This colorful style of painting in miniature developed during a period of rebirth, or renaissance, of Hindu literature beginning in the fourteenth century. Artists used symbolism to depict certain religious themes, and often illustrated classic works of literature such as the *Mahabharata* and the *Ramayana*, famous Hindu epic poems. A bit like folk art, the Rajput school was known to illustrate a variety of Hindu gods as well as animals and people. Colors had specific meanings, and all of these works were highly ornate and contained a narrative, that is, each painting told a story. Rajput painting survived until the occupation of India by the British who directly influenced the arts of India.

The Arts of Islam

Since the late 700s, when Islam arrived on the south Asian subcontinent, traditions of that faith have strongly influenced the architecture of this land from its

The Faisal Mosque in Islamabad was designed by renowned Turkish architect Vedat Dalokay and named after King Faisal of Saudi Arabia, who contributed most of its $50 million cost. It represents an eight-faceted desert tent supported on four minarets. The complex also houses an Islamic Research Center, library, museum, lecture hall, and offices of the faculty of the Islamic University.

beginning to the present. Mosques dominate the landscape where Muslims gather to pray on Fridays and to worship.

Archaeologists have recently uncovered the remains of what is believed to be the first mosque built on the Indian subcontinent, a site known as Mansura, located about 40 miles (60 kilometers) northeast of Hyderabad in the Sindh province.

Towers and minarets spring skyward from these mosques, which often contain large courtyards to hold the huge gatherings of Muslims who stand in lines to recite their prayers. Often decorated with white and gold domes, mosques feature colonnades of arches whose tops reflect the shapes of the domes and line the inner gathering space. In Peshawar, for example, three fluted domes cover the prayer hall and balconies that decorate the twin minarets of the Mahabat Khan Mosque, built during the Mughal Empire and later renovated in the twentieth century.

The most modern mosque in Pakistan stands in Islamabad, a city designed to be the international showplace of the nation. The Faisal Mosque stands prominently at the northwestern end of Shah Faisal Avenue. Four angular minarets rise 270 feet (90 meters) toward the sky at the corners of the prayer hall, which was designed to resemble the tents of the desert dwellers of Arabia. The main courtyard features a marble floor. The Faisal Mosque is reported to be the largest in the world, with room for 10,000 to 15,000 people in the prayer hall and 85,000 in the courtyard.

Colorful mosaics decorate the outsides and insides of both mosques and tombs, or mausoleums. In Hyderabad and in Sukkur, both cities in the Sindh province, stand two well-preserved tombs built for Sindh rulers in the 1700s. Blue, white, and red tiles decorate their tall walls and archways.

The men pictured here work at a carpet factory in Lahore. Carpet weaving as an art form dates back to the reign of Akbar the Great, ruler of the Mughal Empire. However, it was not until the East India Company opened the doors for European export that carpet production was commercialized. Carpets produced in Pakistan today are more innovative in design than contemporary Persian carpets. Pakistani manufacturers are always adding new designs or reviving traditional ones.

Across Pakistan, mausoleums from the Mughal period and earlier highlight the landscape. Other tombs also provide an opportunity to display the Islamic influence on Pakistani architecture. In Hyderabad stands the eighteenth-century tomb of Ghulam Nabi Kalhora, a ruler of Sindh. In Bhit Shah, a small town south of Hala in Sindh, the brilliant blue tiles of the tomb of Shah Abdul Latif, a celebrated mystic and poet born in 1689, attract visitors. Blue-tiled columns of a mausoleum rise above Uch in the southern Punjab province.

A modern interpretation of the Islamic tomb is the dome-topped, sand-colored rectangle of Muhammad Ali Jinnah, the father of Pakistan. It stands on a plaza at the northeastern end of Jinnah Road in Karachi, the huge port on the Arabian coast. So common are tombs and mosques in Pakistan that travel writers sometimes refer to Pakistan's small towns as places surrounded by dozens of old tombs and mosques.

Modern Architecture

Modern buildings similar to those in large cities around the world decorate the skylines of Pakistan's metropolitan cities. Islamabad is the showplace of modern buildings, as much of the city was built in the 1960s and 1970s. In addition to its world-famous mosque, the government buildings of this planned city reflect an image of the country its founders hoped to create. The angles of the Supreme Court building demonstrate the use of geometry in Islamic design. The Presidential Palace, the Parliament Building, and the Federal Secretariat are all white, low-rise, expansive structures. The Greek company known as Doxiadis Associates designed much of Islamabad.

In Karachi, Pakistan's largest city, modern hotels rise up next to office buildings built while Great Britain ruled India. While some buildings reflect Pakistani culture with the use of arches and lights, many mimic the angular appearance common in large urban hotels around the world.

The Modernist Period

Pakistan has a thriving modern art community. Since independence in 1947, Pakistani artists have sought to express their new roles as citizens of a new nation. Many worked to discover a difference between their shared history with India and their own national identities.

The Wazir Khan Mosque in Lahore is reputedly one of the most beautiful in Pakistan. It was built in AD 1634 by Hakim Ali-ud-din, also known as Wazir Khan, who was governor of the area during the reign of Shah Jahan. This mosque is famous for its interior and exterior frescoes of Arabesque paintings.

This painting on a truck is typical of the inspirational and expressive art found in Pakistan. There is an explicit order and hierarchy of values expressed in truck painting. The highest part of the truck is reserved for images that celebrate Islam, such as verses of the Koran painted in calligraphy. The truck's rear is normally reserved for one large motif that is painted on separate wooden planks. Only when the wooden planks are inserted correctly does the picture appear.

Abdur Rahman Chugtai was Pakistan's leading painter at the time of independence. He was concerned that much of the art of his people and their mosques, tombs, and temples were distinctly a part of India. Chugtai and other painters of the time turned to the geography of the new Pakistan, the mountains and the deserts, and to its Muslim culture, for inspiration.

As the years went by and Pakistan's political leaders worked to build a nation, artists explored their shared heritage with India. Allah Bux found inspiration in the stories of Buddha and in the painting styles familiar to Europeans and Americans through the works of Pablo Picasso and modern French painters.

In the 1960s, Sadequain Naqvi, a Pakistani who lived many years in Paris, blended calligraphy into his works, using "word art" to create a mural around the tops of the walls of the Lahore Museum.

By the end of the twentieth century, artists such as Jamal Shah, Fizza Haider, and Aamir Khatri were turning to the landscape and people of rural Pakistan for inspiration. They

Embroidery in Pakistan is a popular handicraft that has become a commercial activity as well as a household one. Every region of the country has its own distinct designs. The National Institute of Folk and Traditional Heritage was founded in 1974 to encourage this tradition and ensure the future of this important national folk art.

also explored the contrast between the modern world and more ancient traditions. The graphic arts of advertising and publishing also became important in Pakistan as modern technology brought mass media to the nation.

Folk Art

Art is an important part of everyday life in Pakistan, and its people use it to bring meaning to their lives. Folk art, or the art of the people, is not reserved for art galleries and museums. Three areas where the Pakistani fondness for decorating their lives is best shown are in embroidery, rugs, and even long-haul trucks.

These young Pakistani girls are adorned with traditional beadwork. Many women and girls adorn their clothing with extensive embroidery, beadwork, or jewelry. Pakistanis are well known for their intricately embroidered and beaded textiles. The Pashtun, for example, are known for their use of small, circular pieces of felt or leather decorated with seed beads, shells, and mirrors.

Women of various ethnic tribes embellish their clothing with fine needlework and embroidery. Women do most of this work by hand on traditional fabrics of cotton and wool, or perhaps silk, using silk or cotton thread. Machine embroidery, however, is becoming a tool of wealthy women who can afford the machines. Most Pakistani women, though, use needles, threads, and fabrics to decorate dresses, hats,

Ceramics of terra-cotta pots, figurines, or toys that resemble the 3,000-year-old ones from Mohenjo-Daro and Harappa are reproduced throughout Pakistan. Each province of the country has its own distinct colors and designs of glazed pottery. Blue and white tiles of Multan, for instance, or the paper-thin black clay wares of Bahawalpur, are among the most popular examples of Pakistani pottery.

scarves, clothing, and gifts. Punjabi women decorate shawls, known as *phulkari*, made of cotton that has been dyed a deep cinnamon color with yellow and white silk threads. Muslims and Sikhs use geometric shapes where their Hindu relatives in India decorate their shawls with human and animal figures. In Baluchistan, women embroider long dresses and children's shirts with patterns handed down from generation to generation. Women in the Chitral district stitch patterns of rams' horns on their men's woolen coats while the Kalash decorate woolen hoods with cowrie shells.

The nomadic Baluchi are known around the world for their weaving style. As travelers herding their animals across the arid plateau of western Pakistan, eastern Iran, and Afghanistan, they need to be able to pack up their goods and haul them easily on their own backs or by camel back. Women weave thick and thin pile rugs in deep blues, browns, reds, and blacks on looms secured to the ground with ropes and pegs. Their designs include leaves, flowers, and animals. Women often weave rugs in patterns that were memorized as

girls. In addition to ground covering, the Baluchi use these rugs as tablecloths, saddle covers, and bags.

Long-haul trucks that carry goods across Pakistan would look much like the semitrucks in the United States except for the elaborate paintings that decorate their panels and roofs. Folk artists paint their trucks in workshops on the outskirts of Pakistan's major cities. Using bright colors they paint scenery, religious figures, and popular sports heroes before adding metal trim, colorful chains, and Arabic calligraphy. Some truckers will even have crafters build special wooden additions to the roof of the cab, giving a truck the look of a throne traveling down the road.

This man stands next to his ornately decorated truck. Transportation vehicles in Pakistan, including vans, buses, trucks, and even motor scooters are often remarkable works of art. Many are painted with poetry verses, flowers, birds, mountain landscapes, movie stars, and passages from the Koran. This vehicle is also equipped with musical horns and laminated photos of General Ayub, or the Aga Khan.

THE LITERATURE AND MUSIC OF PAKISTAN

8

C enturies-old traditions as well as modern life blend to form the literature and music of Pakistan. The people of this land belong to ethnic groups with deeply rooted oral and musical forms. While they treasure the poetry that has been passed down to them for generations, Pakistanis also admire modern authors.

Literature

Muslims do not revere classic works of Indian literature, such as the *Mahabharata* and *Ramayana*—once celebrated by Hindus living in the region. These works are considered religious and often celebrate a multitude of Hindu gods. Muslim Pakistanis instead study the Koran and have infused classic native stories with Islamic themes and culture beginning in the eighth century.

Pakistani authors have struggled to become writers of literature. Some insisted upon the separation of their present and future from a shared past with India. Others claimed that they could not separate their literary traditions from that history even though the two nations were now separated.

This man (*left*) beats on drums in Karachi. Folk music in Pakistan serves not only as a form of entertainment but also as a ritual part of festivals and celebrations. The playing of folk music is often a group event with various people joining in to play instruments. This miniature Indian painting from a *Ragamala (*book of music and poetry, *above*) dates from 1660. Indian miniatures were rarely framed or hung on walls. Instead the paintings were made to study their delicacy and content. Miniatures were painted in order to provide the viewer with a means to heighten his or her intelligence and imagination.

The manuscript shown on this page is from an incomplete anthology of Persian poetry dating from the sixteenth century. The verses are written in the central frames that are gold lined, with comments detailed in the margins. Persian poetry was often written in an Arabic script known as *Nasta'liq*, which is an elegant and fluid writing style popular for translating literary works.

Today, Pakistan still faces tribal divisions. Writers use Urdu, a language now more common in India than Pakistan. Some, such as Alamgir Hashmi, a renowned modern poet who grew up in Lahore, write in English, along with Urdu and Punjabi. Each of these major languages has its own literary tradition. As Pakistan matures as a nation, writers, publishers, and critics work to discover opportunities for people to create literature in many of the languages spoken by its people.

Urdu poetry is said to be some of the most passionate love poetry ever written. In the 1600s and 1700s, Urdu evolved into a poetic language used to share the depths of emotional struggle. That poetry developed through the centuries in northeastern India.

First came the *ghazal*, a structured form of love poetry, written in six to twenty-six paired lines. This poetry appealed to people of all classes. Festivals of poets, called *musha'eras*, became common. At these festivals, people gathered for days to hear their favorite poets recite ghazals. Shamsuddin Mohammad Vali (1668–1741) wrote in this style and was much revered in his time. Later, Indian and Islamic ideas merged to form *thumri* poetry.

In the late nineteenth century, as the Muslims of India began their struggle for freedom from both British rule and the Hindu majority, Urdu poetry served as an artistic way to express the conflict. Allama Muhammad Iqbal (1877–1938) was a philosopher, thinker, and leader who used his gift for poetry to influence Muslims in thinking about a separate homeland. He is considered one of the greatest Urdu poets of Pakistan. Other

The text of the *Sri Bhagavata Purana* is written in Sanskrit. The *Sri Bhagavata Purana* is an elaborately illustrated text that mixed legends, myths, biographies of great leaders, allegories, and chronicles of historical events in an attempt to explain the principles of religion to the common people. Sanskrit is an ancient, classical language of India and Hinduism.

modern poets and fiction writers have followed, including Hanif Kureishi, Sara Suleri, and Ahmed Ali.

Other Languages

Writers in all of the major languages of Pakistan are working to build the literature of their people. They seek to elevate the artistry of their language above the spoken story or ages-old epic and write what some would call high literature.

Sindhi, the language of the Sindh people of southeastern Pakistan, has a long tradition of religious poetry. Increasingly, Sindhi artists are turning to this language to help them establish their own cultural identity within Pakistan.

Punjabi has long been the language of folktales on the Indian subcontinent. As the first language spoken by most of the people of Pakistan, Punjabi is increasingly becoming the first language that poets, novelists, and dramatists choose to express their ideas.

Music

Traditional music, largely different for each of Pakistan's major tribal groups, plays an important role in national and local ceremonies. Modern popular music is also heard frequently in Pakistan's cities and is influenced by worldwide trends in Europe, Asia, and the United States. Pakistan has its own growing rock and roll, and popular music scene, but many people listen to the music of other countries.

The rural areas of Pakistan are home to the country's traditional musicians. These players learn the songs and styles passed down from one generation to the next. People sing and play a variety of instruments such as the *tambura*, a stringed instrument like a lute, or a *tabla*, which is a pair of drums.. Professional musicians play traditional instruments, too, such as the *dholak*, a long drum with a head on each end, or the *alghoza*, a two-reed flute. It is very common in the rural villages for women to gather and sing songs that celebrate special occasions. At weddings women sing to the bride songs that they learned from their mothers. Each step in the ceremony is honored with its own composition. In some parts of Pakistan, women are not allowed to sing in public. In other parts,

Qawwali

Known as the national music of Pakistan, *qawwali* is devotional music made popular by mystic Sufi poets. This rhythmic chanting and repeated verse is most often heard to celebrate the death anniversaries of certain Sufi saints. The Sufis believe that chanting and music brings them closer to Allah. Usually qawwali is spoken in Urdu, Punjabi, or Persian (Farsi) and can sometimes be improvisational, which means that the Sufi musicians and singers arrange the music and words as they perform. Most of these performances occur at Sufi shrines or festivals.

This miniature painting shows the religious dance of initiation and is from the poems by Hafiz ash Shirrazi. Pakistan has a long tradition of art and poetry. Qawwali, devotional music, is one of its most revered forms. These songs are set to music and accompanied by hand-clapping. The *ghazal* is another lyric form of rhythmic poetry that is set to music.

Qawwali music utilizes stringed instruments called *sarangis*, or harmoniums, percussion instruments like pianos. Most bands have several male singers—females are not permitted to play qawwali music—and at least two musicians. Pakistan's most famed qawwali singer is Nusrat Fateh Ali Khan, known in Pakistan as the King of Kings. Khan, who passed away in 1997, released several full-length compositions and was internationally recognized.

This Baluchi folk singer performs at a public gathering. Nomadic Baluchi tribes are united by their language and music. For the most part, the Baluchi tribal music owes its development to an ethnic group called *osta*, meaning "masters." The origins of the group are unknown, but they are responsible for merging the ancestral music skills of several nomadic tribes. Today's Baluchi musicians pride themselves on having a prestigious lineage.

particularly cities, women have become popular entertainers.

Traditional Pakistani music follows the monophonic, or one sound, pattern. It has only a melody and no harmony. That sound may be sung or played on an instrument. Rhythm is important and can offer more variety to the music. At *Lok Virsa*, the National Institute of Folk Heritage holds an annual festival in October each year where traditional musicians gather to perform for large crowds.

Musicians are turning to high-tech ways to combine traditional sounds with popular music. Urban Pakistanis have easy access to the music of the United States and other lands in retail stores and even over the Internet.

They are adding their sound to that international mix, with amplified stringed instruments and drums, upbeat rhythms, and even harmonies.

Street singers from the Punjab province perform a traditional Marasi dance. Before 1947, Pakistan's devotional and popular music was similar to Indian styles. Pakistan has now developed its own musical identity. Because the culture places a great importance on poetry, partly because of the emphasis put on the Koran as the literal word of Allah, the poems of Muhammad Iqbal (1877–1938) are often regarded as themes in Pakistan's popular national music.

FAMOUS FOODS AND RECIPES OF PAKISTAN

9

Even in their kitchens, Pakistanis reveal the variety of their complex heritage. Each wave of invaders has imprinted its influences on the cuisine of Pakistan. The preparation of foods and specialty dishes popular with Persians, Mughals, and Arabs—such as grilled and stewed meats, stews, and *tikka kababs* (made in a tandoor oven)—have all blended to form the cuisine that is now one of the country's acclaimed cultural attributes. Spicy hot to sugary sweet delicacies, basic breads, and complicated blends of meat and pastry comprise its flavorful and hearty fare.

From their shared ancestry, Pakistanis developed a love of spicy foods, much like Indian dishes, though some claim Pakistan's versions are a bit milder than their Indian counterparts. Recipes that once originated with the Mughals have a spice blend that is somewhat distinctive. These dishes often rely on a unique mixture of saffron, cardamom, and roasted sesame or poppy seeds. A Pakistani delight that was once a favorite of the Mughal emperor Akbar is *haleem*, a meat dish prepared with seven

Young street vendors *(left)* sell corn on the cob. Agriculture is the backbone of Pakistan's economy. More than 70 percent of the country's population depends directly or indirectly on agriculture for its livelihood. Hunza women *(above)* sort freshly picked apricots and arrange them on circular mats for sun drying. It is believed that the apricots grown by the Hunza Valley people keep them strong and healthy. These people support themselves almost solely by farming the land and raising animals.

A man crushes spices and sells them on the street. Spices are aromatic substances derived from vegetable plants. Like India, Pakistan is also home to some of the finest spices in the world. Heating spices—whether toasting them or frying them in oil—greatly enhances their flavor. Grinding whole spices also retains their freshness. Pakistanis use spices in cooking, as a fragrance, and as preservatives.

grains including rice, wheat, and lentils. Other popular flavors include turmeric, a rhizome of the ginger family; coriander; cilantro or Chinese parsley; and *amchoor*, made from sour, unripe mangoes.

Many of Pakistan's common spicy meat dishes, such as *korma*, are served with a side of yogurt, or *raita*, often to cool the palate. A distinct difference between the Muslims of Pakistan and India's Hindus is that Muslims do not eat pork. Though Indians are largely vegetarian, Pakistanis eat a variety of meats other than pork. Muslims often request *halal* meats, or meats that are slaughtered in a specific way according to the laws of Islam. Holiday menus may include such dishes as *sevayyan* and *sheer khorma*, puddings prepared from vermicelli. Sweets such as *barfi*, or fudge, are also popular during the holidays.

Meat is the center of most Pakistani dishes, and chicken, beef, and mutton provide cooks with alternate central ingredients. Chefs add a wide variety of spices and flavorings to ground meat and either grill it as patties or weave it onto a skewer to

This woman of the Magwar tribe dries red chilies in front of her mud house. Chili peppers are dried berry fruits that are used as spices to improve the flavor of food. Dundicut, a type of chili, is the traditional hot pepper of Pakistan, where it has been cultivated for years. A single crushed dundicut pepper adds heat and flavor to several meals.

make more portable meals. Popular sides and garnishes often include fried onions, raisins, or roasted cashews, pistachios, and almonds.

The smell and sound of meat such as *bhuna gosht* sizzling in hot oil, fill many of Pakistan's narrow streets. Deep fat frying is a common method of food preparation in many homes and bazaar eateries. Meat stews simmer overnight to make Pakistan's famous *nihari*, an important breakfast dish of beef chunks with ginger, onions, chilis, coriander, and lime juice. In Karachi and in some southern towns, people often add seafood to their diet. One popular seafood entrée is a seafood curry called *machli ka salan*.

Bread is so common in Pakistan that it accompanies every meal. A yeast-free flat bread, or one that does not rise, sometimes serves as a spoon for meals. This flat bread is called *chapati* or *roti*. Prepared from a mix of wheat flour and water, this dough is kneaded together before cooking. Pakistanis form the dough into small balls and then roll each ball out flat to make a circle. They then fry the bread on a hot griddle.

Naan or *nan* is the most popular raised bread in Pakistan. This light bread includes milk and sugar to make it sweet, and yeast and baking powder to make it rise. After mixing the ingredients, bakers let the dough rise for three hours, then shape it into balls, flatten the balls into round disks, and bake the dough in a hot oven. Naan comes out looking like the crust of a thick pan pizza. It is often served as a side dish for many meals in Pakistan.

Pakistani chefs add zest to their lamb, chicken, and seafood dishes with a variety of spices such as green chili peppers, black pepper, nutmeg, and cinnamon. Like

Lemon Chicken
Serves 4 to 6

Pakistani cooks like to sauté chicken in fresh lemon juice, or make a fried version using a lemon paste spread over the meat followed by a coating of flour.

1 whole chicken, cut up, or 6 boneless,
   skinless chicken breasts
1 teaspoon minced garlic
1 teaspoon minced ginger
Juice of 2 big lemons (3 to 4 tablespoons)
1 tablespoon olive oil
Salt and black pepper to taste
Coriander leaves for garnish (optional)

Directions:
Rinse chicken pieces clean and pat dry. Place them in a large baking dish. In a small bowl, blend together the garlic, ginger, lemon juice, and olive oil. Pour this mixture over the chicken pieces, using tongs to evenly coat pieces. Marinate in the refrigerator for several hours, or prepare at once for a milder flavor. Grill the chicken outdoors for 20 to 25 minutes on a charcoal or gas grill. Using a medium heat setting, turn the pieces every 4 to 5 minutes until they're fully and evenly cooked.

yogurt, a piece of favorite bread and a big helping of rice help ease the heat of certain spice combinations.

Groves of mangoes, guavas, lemons, apricots, and other fruits grow in the fertile irrigated lands of Punjab. Bananas also thrive in the subtropical regions of this land, located in the foothills of Pakistan's northern mountains. Dessert is often based

Mixed Fruit Shake
Serves 4

Try this basic recipe to capture a sense of the importance of fruit and yogurt in Pakistani cuisine.

17½ ounces (500 grams) vanilla, cherry,
    or strawberry yogurt
2 oranges (or the juice of three oranges)
2 ripe bananas
12 to 14 fresh or frozen strawberries
14 to 16 fresh (pitted) or frozen cherries

Directions:
Spoon the yogurt into a blender. Peel the oranges, removing as much of the white, stringy pith as possible. Break the oranges into pieces and put them in the blender, or add the juice. Peel the bananas, break them into small chunks, and add them to the blender. Add the fresh or frozen strawberries and cherries. (If you use fresh fruit, clean it thoroughly, removing the stems and pits.) Blend on medium high until smooth. You may need to stop the blender at times to mix the ingredients with a plastic spoon.

When smooth, pour into four tall glasses and serve. Optional: Garnish with fresh fruit chunks.

on fruit mixed with milk and yogurt to make a pudding or sorbet, a fruit-based frozen dessert. Fruits are also the basic ingredients in Pakistan's chutneys, relishes popular as condiments with meat and bread.

A street vendor fries *parathas*, a common breakfast food. It is a flat cake fried in oil and usually eaten with an omelette or fried egg. Sometimes it will have a vegetable filling. Many popular Pakistani foods are fried in large quantities of oil, a practice that tends to destroy vitamins and minerals.

Street Vendors

Many Pakistanis claim that their nation is the "street food" capital of the world. The bazaars of cities and towns, famous for their goods and wares for sale—rugs, jewelry, embroidered caps, and fabrics—are filled with small stalls selling foods of every kind, from various single ingredients to a snack on the run. These finger foods might include *pakora*, deep-fried dough balls, or *bhajia*, batter-fried vegetables. Other common products to buy from street vendors are refreshments such as *chai*, or tea. Chai is offered to guests in private homes as well as in many shops. Tea in Pakistan is served hot, with sugar, and is normally infused with warm milk and spices such as nutmeg, cinnamon, cloves, and cardamom. Sometimes, in cities such as Baltistan, the chai is churned with butter and is known as Tibetan tea. The drinking of alcoholic beverages is prohibited in Islam, and therefore prohibited in Pakistan.

Pakistan has a rich cuisine, but it is also the home of many rural people who have very little to eat each day. Between 32 and 40 percent of Pakistanis live in

poverty, one of the highest poverty rates in the world. For them, basic foods are made of wheat and rice and rarely contain meat. If they farm in Baluchistan or southern Sindh, they grow few crops on very poor soil, but eat what they harvest. Many city poor do not earn enough money to buy much of the street food or the fresh food sold in city markets.

Fast food, like the type known to people living in the United States and Europe, has also come to Pakistan. McDonald's, for example, opened its first restaurant in Pakistan in Lahore in 1998 and now also has a restaurant in Faisalabad. McDonald's created three specialty sandwiches for its Pakistani customers: Chatpata Chicken Roll, Chicken 'n Chutni Burger, and Spicy Chicken Burger.

The Pakistanis pictured here are enjoying breakfast in a hut. *Nihari* breakfasts are popular since they provide sustenance throughout long days. This morning meal consists of chunks of beef, which are cooked overnight in a metal pot, along with oil, chilies, and spices. Portions of bone marrow, brain, kidney, or liver can be added to the mixture. Because Pakistanis believe the left hand is unclean, they eat only with their right hands.

DAILY LIFE AND CUSTOMS IN PAKISTAN

10

T he lifestyle of a Pakistani family largely depends on where in Pakistan they reside and the economy of that region. Most Pakistanis, no matter where they live, will wake in the early morning and pray, practicing one of the tenets of Islam.

In Pakistan, traditional, conservative Muslims live their lives according to their understandings of the teachings of the Koran, even if their neighbors might have different interpretations of the holy book and live their lives differently. While most people in Pakistan follow the tenets of Islam, some do not.

The face of Islam in Pakistan is changing. The way in which family members express their faith is also changing. A man may choose to live a very traditional religious life. His wife, unwed daughters, and daughters-in-law will live together in rooms separate from where the men reside. These women rarely leave their homes (a practice known as *purdah*) and do not mix with visitors. In this family, the father and mother arrange the marriages of their children and their daughters go to live with their husbands' families. Other Muslims may choose a more modern life in which men and women live together and girls and boys of all ages play and are educated together.

Pakistani women *(left)* prefer clothing with rich designs and bright colors. Women's dress normally includes a *salwar kameez* and a *dupatta*. The salwar kameez is the long shirt and skirt worn from neck to ankles, and the dupatta is the scarf worn over the head and wrapped around the shoulders. In the town of Multan, a public bus *(above)* is overcrowded with people. Safe travel in Pakistan is subject to weather, road conditions, and sheer luck. Bandits tend to prey on buses and trains, and many of the public transportation vehicles are old and dilapidated. Areas within the North-West Frontier Province are designated tribal regions and are beyond the normal jurisdiction of law enforcement. Traveling within this province can be extremely hazardous.

Child Labor

Child labor, especially hard work that damages a child's body, is still common in Pakistan, though human rights advocates have begun to address this long-standing problem. In some factories, children sit in poorly lit rooms stitching soccer balls or knotting hand-woven rugs, or spend their day packing mud into brick forms. Some children work fourteen hours or more each day with few breaks. Many also work long hours in rice or wheat fields.

In 2000, more than 7.2 million Pakistani children between the ages of ten and nineteen were employed rather than educated, according to the International Labor Organization of the United Nations (UN). Estimates also report that 1.4 million children under the age of ten are employed in Pakistan. Since 1994, Pakistan's government has participated in efforts by UN organizations to end child labor, including passing restrictive laws that it struggles to enforce.

Iqbal Masih was a Pakistani child who spent more than six years working in hot, cramped conditions in a carpet factory for as many as fourteen hours a day, tying small pieces of thread to carpets. If the workers tried to leave, they would often be chained to the floor. Although Masih escaped this life with the help of Pakistan's child labor laws and the Bonded Labor Liberation Front, he was shot and killed on April 16, 1995, in a random act of violence. Children and students around the world have kept up Masih's fight and are now helping to end Pakistan's child labor problem through education.

Daily life in Pakistan is also evolving. Since its beginnings as a nation in 1947, Pakistan's government has struggled to support itself and its people. The forces of poverty, illiteracy, human rights, and technology are all altering the lifestyles of Pakistanis. The government and private sector are each working to improve the lives of Pakistanis who do not make enough money to feed themselves or build adequate shelters.

A Pakistani worker puts clay into a brick mold at a factory in Bahawalpur. Young children sometimes go to work instead of to school because of the family's financial needs. Child labor is used by many industries throughout the country.

Modern machinery is changing how Pakistanis work and find entertainment. Opportunities are expanding beyond traditional agricultural positions to jobs in manufacturing, shipbuilding, engineering, medicine, and education. The physical challenges of many jobs—such as making bricks by hand—are slowly fading from the everyday lives of the people of Pakistan. Though some people, including children and young adults, spend most of each day working long hours in hot clay quarries to make bricks, efforts to eliminate such hardships have now taken shape.

Concerned individuals from Pakistan and around the world are seeking solutions to these and other major problems around the clock. Educators are working to teach children to read and write. Pakistan is today trying to improve its placement on the chart

A Hunza woman pulls wool for spinning. Although Pakistani women are increasingly gaining rights in modern society, women in both rural and urban communities are still treated like chattel, meaning they are either "given" or "acquired" through arranged marriages. No woman, even with an independent career in the city, can set up a home on her own without the *saya*—literally shade or protection—of a man.

of the world's most illiterate countries. In 1998, the literacy rate among boys was about 56 percent, and even higher for girls, a statistic the Pakistani government is struggling to change.

The Role of Women

World news organizations and human rights groups have shown the challenges that Pakistan faces to improve the lives of its female citizens, many of whom live more difficult lives than men do. But Pakistan is home to some of today's most emancipated females. Female Pakistanis can hold government offices and can become doctors, lawyers, social workers, bankers, or business owners. The problem is that many women lack the education to hold professional positions. Most women living in Pakistan choose more traditional roles such as staying at home and raising a family, a fact that many Westerners attribute to their strict adherence to traditional religious values. The fact is, however, that Islam does not forbid women from entering the workforce. Islam actually preaches equality for women, including the right to an equal education and the right for women to own property. In many cases, however, various community and tribal laws take precedence over traditional Islamic law, or *shari'ah*. Tribal tradition in many parts of Pakistan, particularly rural areas, keeps women and girls from learning to read and write, from holding jobs, and even from leaving their homes. In some cases, Pashtun women are not permitted to inherit property, they retain no rights after they are married, they cannot ask for a divorce, and they have little influence about their own belongings.

Urban Life

More than a dozen of Pakistan's cities have populations that exceed 200,000 people, while other cities' numbers soar into the millions. More than eleven million people live in Karachi, an international shipping port on the Arabian Sea and capital of the Sindh province. High-rise apartment buildings, business centers, manufacturing plants, and miles of docks have brought wealth and people to this harbor city.

In Lahore, home to more than six million Pakistanis, the wealthy residents visit city parks and gardens preserved from the Mughal dynasty. The poor residents make do with mud huts, exploring the city for work and cooling off by swimming in the city's large canals. Islamabad, unlike Lahore, is a new city that was planned beginning in 1961. Islamabad, known as the abode of Islam, boasts millions of trees and low-level buildings that do not block the beauty of the city's many vistas. It has an airy feeling with

This view of the Old City of Lahore shows its splendor. The second-largest city in Pakistan, Lahore is regarded as the cultural, artistic, and architectural center of Pakistan. Over the past few years, Lahore has become a busy metropolis with factories supporting Pakistan's economy but contributing to its growing pollution. Still, some sections of the city retain its essence as the center of the Mughal Empire. Gardens, mosques, and parks add to its appeal, as does the bazaar of the Old City where master craftsmen create masterpieces of copper, brass, silver, and textiles.

This Pakistani man wears a traditional turban. Traditionally styled long turbans, or perhaps two twined together with one end hanging loose, are common in Pakistan, while Muslim religious elders wear turbans that are colorful or white based on legends that Muhammad wore a white turban.

open spaces and wide, modern highways. Rawalpindi, unlike its neighboring city of Islamabad, was founded in the fourteenth century and later modernized by the British. Characterized by its noisy, fast-paced environment, Rawalpindi is peppered with shops, bazaars, and street vendors who sell everything from brass and copper wares to beautifully embroidered cloth. The city is actually famous for its shopping, especially in the section known as the Old City. Few cars enter these old bazaars where streets are normally too narrow. Television and movie stars attract attention on the huge wall murals that decorate structural facades.

Traditional styles of dress are also more relaxed in Pakistan's urban centers and are subject to more individual interpretation. Men may wear turbans, the loose-fitting pants or *pyjama*, with a *kurta*, or long shirt that hangs to the knees, but may also don khaki trousers and shirts or business suits. Women in Western-styled attire are also common. Others wear the *salwar*, or baggy pants with gathered ankles covered by the *salwar kameez*, or loosely fitting tunic. Some women may be covered from head to toe in the *burka* or may just wear a head-covering shawl. Both men and women are fond of jewelry and often wear necklaces, bracelets, and rings as well as headpieces, earrings, and anklets.

Rural Communities

Most people living in Pakistan's villages are faced with a difficult life filled with long hours of labor with little compensation. It is in these tribal communities that the traditions of Pakistan's ethnic groups remain the strongest.

The Baluchi are still somewhat nomadic. Many live in tents and follow their herds of sheep, goats, and cattle to traditional watering areas in their dry, semidesert province. Women tend to the household and raise children. They gather

firewood and water and help with the herds of livestock. Men tend the flocks.

In Sindh villages, people live in mud-brick houses—one-room homes for poorer families, or several rooms and a latrine for wealthier landowners. Those who live near the Indus River work the fields of wheat, corn, rice, and cotton. Others who live in the deserts to the east and west of the river tend flocks of camels, goats, and sheep.

The populations of Pashtun, the cooler mountainous regions of northeastern Pakistan, and Punjab, the agricultural region of eastern Pakistan, are decreasing. Fewer people each year live in these rural communities; instead they are migrating to Pakistan's cities.

Sheep raising in Pakistan is an integral part of its agricultural industry. Sheep and goats constitute an overwhelming majority of the livestock population. They are raised in irrigated areas where vast land provides pastures. Approximately 24.2 million sheep and goats are raised throughout the country for a variety of purposes.

Recreation

People of all ages in Pakistan play the games their Indian ancestors played as well as games they learned from the British, such as cricket, field hockey, and squash.

These men are participating in the Gilgit Annual Equestrian Competition. Polo is a popular sport in this northern region of Pakistan. The game originated in central Asia and was developed into a competitive sport by the Persians. Polo contestants in the northern area are known for their daredevil horsemanship. The pace of the game is controlled by music that increases in pitch as the contest continues. Polo horses are admired for their stamina, which may be explained by their diet of mulberries and walnuts.

Cricket, a game played with a ball and a bat, but very different from baseball, almost always draws crowds of enthusiastic fans. Pakistan's national cricket team has been a contender for international championships for years. As American urban cities have a street version of baseball, young Pakistanis pick up sticks in streets and fields to play a street version of cricket called *gulli-danda*.

Field hockey also draws crowds in Pakistan. The national team competes in international tournaments and draws many fans. In fact, Pakistan's field hockey team won gold medals in the Olympics in 1960 and 1968 and was also prominent in the Olympics in the 1970s.

Squash is another popular sport in Pakistan. More of a game for two opponents rather than an entire team, squash is an ancestor

Tent-pegging began in India about 500 years ago as practice to hunt wild boars on horseback. In this competition, the rider charges across the riding arena and attempts to pick up a wooden four-inch block with a sword or lance. If the rider successfully carries the block to the opposite corner, then the player earns a point.

The women in this photograph are from the Kholi tribe and are carrying pots of drinking water on their heads in the Kasbo village in Thar Desert in the Sindh province of Pakistan.

of racquetball that is played on an indoor court. It captured the heart of Pakistanis after independence. Like squash, soccer is also growing in popularity.

Wrestling, in dirt-filled outdoor rings, is a very old sport in Pakistan. Once supported by wealthy landowners in British-ruled India, today wrestling is a favorite event at regional festivals and tribal gatherings.

Sports involving horses also have long histories in this land. Tent-pegging is an old game where riders try to capture pegs firmly planted in the ground. Polo, some experts say, was developed in the Gilgit region and exported to Great Britain when the country ruled India. The British brought horse racing to India and it still thrives in Pakistan, though gambling on the sport is illegal.

In villages and tribes across this land, people often play the games of their clan. The Baluchis and Sindhis play *chauk*, which resembles checkers, but uses cowrie shells as dice to determine moves by players. Children play tag and variations of hopscotch.

Women play a traditional game called *chatti*. Based on the chore of carrying water jugs from the well, the women run across fields in competitive races.

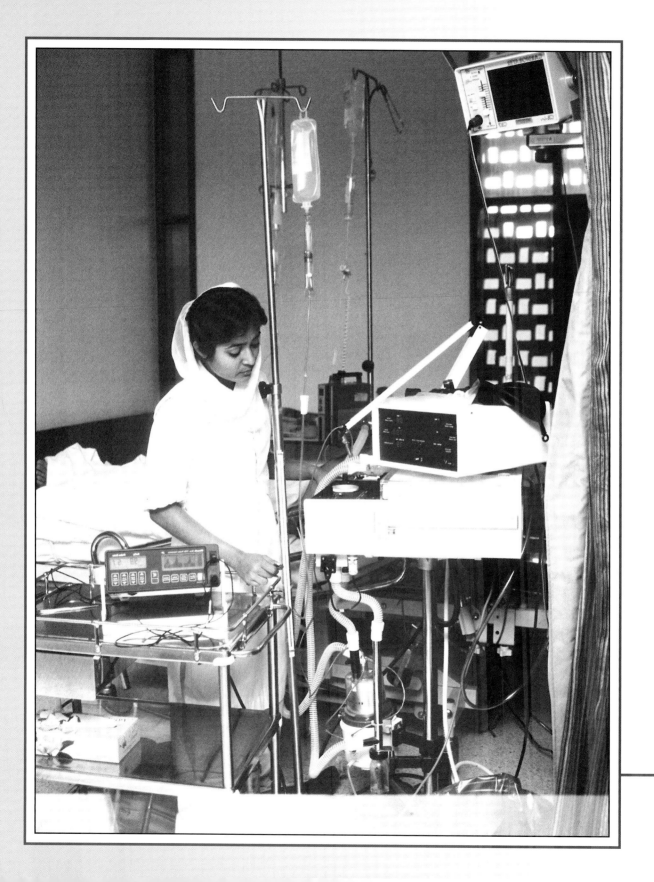

EDUCATION AND WORK IN PAKISTAN

11

Around the world people use literacy, or the ability to read and write, as a measure for how well they are educated. In 2001, 58 percent of Pakistanis aged fifteen and older—or more than 49 million people—could not write a three-sentence paragraph in the language they learned as children. In Pakistan, these figures translate to six out of every ten people who cannot read or write.

While the educational systems are improving in Pakistan, many children, especially those living in rural areas, never gain opportunities to learn literacy skills. Even fewer have the chance to learn mathematics or science. Current statistics show

that up to 40 percent of the children in Pakistan never attend school, while many who begin classes may spend as little as one year in attendance. As a result, most adults in Pakistan cannot read. Without a better, more systemized education system, Pakistan will continue to struggle to create a more industrialized work force that may provide better paying jobs than those in farming and herding livestock. With increased literacy, Pakistan can develop more businesses and services to give people better jobs than making handicrafts, rugs, and mud bricks by hand.

In time, Pakistan's government hopes to improve its citizens' literacy skills. With the support of international aid, leaders in Pakistan are now teaching adults to read in

The professional nurse in this photograph *(left)* works at the Age Kan University Hospital in Karachi, Pakistan. Pakistani children *(above)* read in class. Statistics show that only 34 percent of children who completed primary school could read, and more than 80 percent were unable to write a simple sentence. Although the Pakistani government understands the need of educating its population, it has largely created more schools instead of increasing the quality of existing ones.

Students in this photograph are being taught at a government-run primary school. Although Pakistan's constitution guarantees free and compulsory primary education, this has not yet been achieved throughout the country as only about 40 percent of five- to nine-year olds are enrolled. The curriculum of Pakistan's primary schools consists of classes of Urdu, Sindhi, English, Arabic, and science, which includes mathematics and general science.

special education classes. They are working to provide improved schooling for children across the nation. If they reach their current goals, only 44 percent of adults will be illiterate by 2010. By 2015, Pakistani leaders hope to teach every child to read.

Schools

For the children who do attend classes, many are held in small, ill-equipped village schools where children and teachers meet in tents, such as in Baluchistan. Children who live in Pakistan's cities might go to larger public schools.

Many schools in Pakistan are Islamic religious schools known as madrassas. In these schools, children learn the Koran in Arabic. Some schools teach children to read and write, but many do not. In 2002, the government began to require madrassa administrators to include basic reading and writing in Urdu to help improve the overall quality of education in Pakistan.

These students attend Aithison College in Lahore. Currently there is a need to reform all of Pakistan's twenty-six higher education universities. The ultimate objective of these reforms is to enhance the academic quality of the institutions. The government is enacting steps to provide students and faculty with the material resources to enable a higher intellectual challenge.

According to reports by Pakistan's government, there are 150,963 primary schools, 14,595 middle schools, and 9,808 high schools in Pakistan. Each school's quality can depend on its location and the support the teachers receive from the community. Girls and boys are largely taught separately, and in the schools that are co-ed, girls and boys attend separate classes.

Pakistan has also worked to build universities and currently has 798 arts and science colleges that train people for industrial careers. For higher education, Pakistan has 161 professional colleges and 35 universities.

The wealthier a family is, the more likely it is that its children will attend school. Although public education is free, many poor families cannot afford the pencils and paper, or even the clothes, that their children need to attend. Pakistan's government and citizens want to remove these and other obstacles any family faces. These issues became an important agenda of Pakistan's administration, which

The Pakistan army has a total strength of 520,000 soldiers, larger than that of the United States, with a reserve element of 500,000. Since the founding of Pakistan, the army has been a key component in uniting the nation. Throughout the history of Pakistan, the army has taken control of the government several times to reform it. Pakistan's military currently controls much of its administration.

The Pakistani workers shown in this photograph work in a steel factory. When Pakistan separated from India in 1947, the country began without any industrial base and no institutional, financial, or energy resources. Today, the manufacturing capacity of Pakistan is small, but production is slowly increasing. Important products include processed food, cotton textiles, refined petroleum, and cigarettes.

last changed office in 1999. They understood that increasing literacy skills in the nation would directly translate into a reduced rate of poverty throughout the entire country. In order to solve this problem, the national budget decreased military spending and requested international aid from several world nations including the United States. Pakistan expects to raise the nation's literacy rate by 14 percent by 2010, including offering educational resources to more girls.

Work

Most Pakistanis live in poverty, since only about 28 percent of its citizens are included in its industrialized labor force, according to figures established by Pakistan's government in 2002.

Many people work, but they do not make enough money to buy food and clothing or to seek the

This worker spins wool in a textile factory. Pakistan's textile industry accounts for 65 to 70 percent of its total exports. Pakistan ranks fourth among cotton-producing countries. However, a downward turn of the economy and higher tariffs (taxes) implemented by the government are throwing the textile industry into a crisis.

This man makes a living working in a public laundry service. New technologies like nuclear power and research, vehicle and aircraft assembly, steel mills, cement, and electronics have been incorporated into Pakistan's traditional industries of textile, farming, food processing, and shipping, which were created just after independence.

health care they may need. Like their need to improve Pakistan's educational system, Pakistani leaders are working to improve the overall quality of the lives of their citizens. In fact, poverty has been problematic for much of Pakistan's short history. Corruption has been a serious problem since independence. Government leaders sometimes keep much of the money produced by businesses. Also, sometimes the wealthy demand more services and neglect the poor.

As the twenty-first century began, more than half of the people with jobs in Pakistan worked in agriculture. They grew cotton, wheat, rice, and sugarcane, among other crops. Some of these people work for very little money. They often rely on children to help with the farm, especially those who work on farms where there is little modern machinery.

Centuries of irrigation in Pakistan's Punjab province have converted land that once was desert into very good growing soil. While some farmers own their farms, many work for landlords who hire people to work the fields. Pakistan's government wants more people to own their land, so that the new landowners can keep more of the money earned from crops.

On the coasts of Pakistan, especially along the Arabian Coast, more and more people are becoming seafood farmers. They catch saltwater fish and shrimp, which they in turn sell for high prices to foreign buyers.

Herders in Baluchistan most often raise animals such as cows, sheep, and goats in the rugged, dry hills and mountains. Irrigation has also helped farmers in this semiarid region grow date palms, dates being one of Pakistan's exports. Farmers also grow cotton in irrigated fields to help supply Pakistan's textile mills,

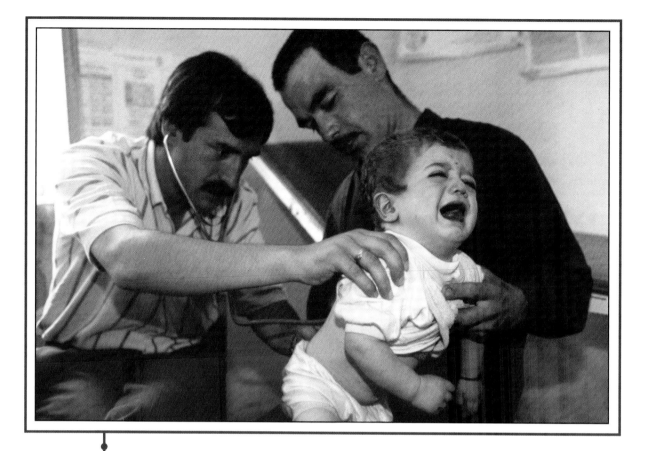

This Pakistani doctor examines a boy at Aliabad Civil Hospital. The government sponsors health care in Pakistan, but over the years, private health care providers have also emerged. The government focuses on primary care and produces affordable drugs for common diseases. Most Pakistanis receive medical attention at clinics or hospitals, but some still visit *hakims*, or herbalists, for traditional medicines.

which produce cotton yarn and fabrics. These mills also employ people in cities such as Faisalabad, Karachi, and Lahore. In smaller villages and towns across the land, people have set up small weaving businesses using looms powered by electricity. These small enterprises are becoming important sources of income.

Some factories also make clothing. Since the 1980s, Pakistan has grown into a leading provider of manufactured clothing. The Textile University opened in Karachi to help train professionals in the textile business. The National College of Arts in Lahore and the Indus Valley School of Art and Architecture in Karachi also train people to design and produce clothing. Even leather garments and furniture, two of the country's fastest-growing industries, are likely to have been made in Pakistan. Many times only the skins of the animals are shipped to other countries where they are turned into various products.

A man assembles a phone at a factory in Haripur. Pakistan's government places a high priority on developing the telecommunications industry, the services of which are growing rapidly. It now provides cellular phones, paging, card-operated telephones, and Internet service.

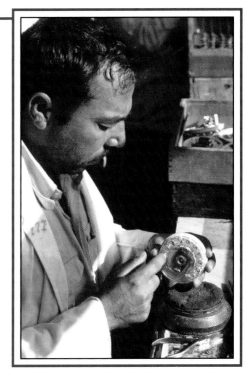

However, Pakistan's crafters also shape that leather into shoes, belts, purses, and even soccer balls, which they also export.

The manufacturing industry has also grown in Pakistan. Workers in foundries in Taxila make metal machine and automobile parts to export around the world. Business entrepreneurs have started some manufacturing plants to make sugar from sugarcane, as well as the production of various medicines.

Well-educated Pakistanis work as doctors, bankers, insurance executives, teachers, and lawyers. As modernization advances and education improves, people will find greater opportunities to work in these professions. In Karachi and Islamabad, for example, more people are entering such professional fields as advertising, television production, journalism, modeling, and sound recording. Civil service jobs are also attracting more people.

Conclusion

The people of Pakistan, its many cultures and its government, began the twenty-first century still working to form the nation their founding fathers had imagined. Many Pakistanis worked to fortify a modern economy, and to bring jobs and education to the land of deserts and high mountains. Others worked to prevent the influences of Western societies from dominating their country. Pakistan's government worked with its neighbors and with nations around the world to help bring peace in the region, yet war with India kept Jammu and Kashmir a divided and dangerous territory. The path to the future, many experts believe, will be a life of opportunity and turmoil. Pakistanis, however, have faith in their God and in their history to guide them. Though still a young nation, Pakistan continues its efforts to fulfill the dream that formed its independent borders and defined its Islamic roots.

PAKISTAN
AT A GLANCE

HISTORY

Pakistan became a nation on August 14, 1947. Great Britain ended its colonial rule of the south Asian subcontinent on that day by signing a treaty that established two separate nations out of the lands it had ruled.

The provinces where most of the people were Muslims became Pakistan. These were located in the northwest and northeast of the subcontinent and called West Pakistan and East Pakistan. The people who lived in the other provinces were mostly Hindu and these provinces became the Republic of India.

The people of West and East Pakistan, separated by 1,000 miles (1,600 kilometers) of the northern part of India, worked to establish their long-distance relationship as a nation during the next two decades. Disagreements over political, cultural, and economic issues eventually led to civil war in 1970. By 1971, East Pakistan separated from West Pakistan and became the nation of Bangladesh.

The land that is now Pakistan has a long history. One of the oldest civilizations developed along the Indus Valley in about 2500 BC. The people of the Indus Valley, or the Harappan civilization, established settlements at the same time as the better known civilizations of Egypt and Mesopotamia. The Indus Valley covered most of Pakistan and parts of eastern India. It included more than 1,500 cities and villages.

After the decline of the Indus Valley civilization by 1700 BC, tribal leaders built smaller kingdoms across the land. At times, strong neighbors sent armies to conquer the tribal and regional leaders. The Persian Empire from what is now Iran ruled the lands from 559 to 330 BC when Alexander the Great of Greece crossed the mountains of Afghanistan and conquered much of the Indus Valley.

The Macedonian (Greek) Empire controlled this land for less than three years, but the influences of the Hellenistic culture remained for centuries. Invaders from central Asia crossed down through the Hindu Kush and Himalaya Mountains in the early part of the second century AD. Islam arrived on the shores of the Arabian Sea, north of the mouth of the Indus River, in AD 710, and soon became a dominant religion on the subcontinent, as were Buddhism and Hinduism.

By 1526, under the leadership of Babur, descendents of Asian invaders established the Mughal Empire, which ruled for more than 300 years until the British Empire gained control of the subcontinent in the mid-1800s.

The government and people of modern Pakistan have struggled since 1947 to make a success of their nation, sometimes under elected democratic governments. At other times, military leaders have established control of the land. In 1999, General Pervez Musharraf took control of the nation in a bloodless coup and became its head of government, an administration that was made official in 2001.

ECONOMY

Pakistan is an impoverished country, but its government is working to improve its economy. At the beginning of the twenty-first century, Pakistan faced an uncertain future. Before Pervez Musharraf took control in 1999, previous governments were in debt to other nations. Musharraf faced an important struggle to decrease that debt so that Pakistan could spend money domestically.

The Musharraf administration has made agreements with the World Bank, the International Monetary Fund, and other lending organizations to restructure that debt. This will give Pakistan time to reorganize future financial responsibilities.

Pakistan's economy is hurt by the fact that more than 40 percent of its people live in poverty. Many Pakistanis are unable to earn enough money to meet the basic necessities of food, clothing, and shelter. To try to solve this problem, the current government has begun a major poverty reduction program.

Government leaders want to decrease military spending in order to invest in Pakistan's human resources. They want to spend more money on educating people and improving human rights. Both of those efforts should improve the skills of the people and increase the money that they will be paid for their work.

The wealthier people of Pakistan have had to pay very few taxes. To improve many conditions in that nation, economists are advising the government to develop programs where the affluent will be faced with increasing taxes. This tax money will help governments pay for the services they provide for society.

Pakistani leaders have often been charged with corruption. They also have been accused of implementing building projects that did not serve the people. Musharraf's administration is struggling to overcome these charges.

Pakistan sees several major challenges to improving its economy. One of the biggest problems is the size of its population. With more than 144.6 million people living in a land the size of Great Britain, which is home to just 59 million people, Pakistan must support a huge growing population. Pakistan's government now hopes to slow that growth rate by encouraging people to have smaller families.

Pakistanis have little security in that they do not save very much money, another trend the government hopes to change. Administrators are working to create a stronger, more trustworthy banking system. If people saved money in national banks, Pakistan would eventually have money—and its earned interest—to invest in building and manufacturing projects.

GOVERNMENT AND POLITICS

Leaders of Pakistan's struggle for independence wanted the new country to become a democratic nation. Pakistan has instead struggled to develop a strong political system, but in its short history has rarely had a democratic government. Pakistan's leadership is instead based on its military power.

The Muslim League, which led the fight for the formation of Pakistan, was not prepared to lead the country in 1947. Muslim League members were well-educated people who had lived in areas that became part of India. They had lived with the principles of majority vote and open government and were used to free discussion and debate. The Muslims of the Pakistani provinces lived in a poor society dominated by strong landowners and conservative religious leaders. These people were not comfortable with the openness and freedom necessary to fulfill the founding fathers' dreams.

Significant conflict between people who wanted strict Islamic law to dominate Pakistan, and those who wanted religion to be separate from the process of governing, prevented the formation of a government until 1956. The third and last constitution was written in 1973.

The huge geographic separation between West Pakistan (the provinces along the Indus Valley) and East Pakistan (the provinces east of India on the Bay of Bengal) caused more problems for Pakistan's development. The people of the two regions had different ideas of how the new nation should form and who should control its government. East Pakistan became Bangladesh in 1971 after a civil war with West Pakistan.

The current government, led by Pervez Musharraf, took power in 1999. Since that time, Pakistan's third constitution has been suspended. Musharraf established an eight-member security council to govern the nation. The administration maintained much of the civil service structure of the Pakistani government. Ministers lead organizations that oversee such social needs as education, local government and rural development, employment, foreign affairs, and agriculture. Musharraf dissolved the Parliament in 1999 as new elections were being planned for 2002. In the provinces, regional governors administer the services provided by the government.

The laws are administered by the Supreme Court. This is made up of a chief justice and thirteen judges. Each province also has a High Court. The number of judges in each varies from fifty in Punjab to six in the North-West Frontier Province. These courts maintain courtrooms where laws under the constitution, the National Assembly, or government order are upheld. Many reflect Islamic religious laws.

The Musharraf government allows political parties to exist. Critics, however, say that the government interprets laws in such ways that party leaders cannot stand for election and some cannot return to Pakistan from exile. The existing parties represent groups struggling for democracy and others who want Pakistan governed by strict interpretations of Islamic law.

Musharraf is now under pressure from Islamic fundamentalists to change his policies. These fundamentalists strongly objected to the help Musharraf gave to the United States in fighting against Afghanistan's Taliban regime following the September 11, 2001, terrorist attacks. Observers agree that Pakistan's government is in a state of turmoil.

TIMELINE

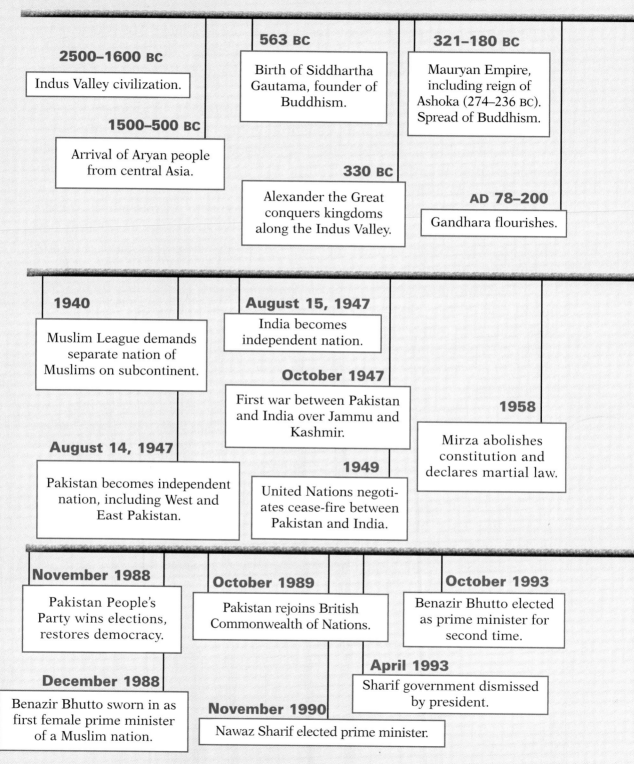

2500–1600 BC

Indus Valley civilization.

1500–500 BC

Arrival of Aryan people from central Asia.

563 BC

Birth of Siddhartha Gautama, founder of Buddhism.

330 BC

Alexander the Great conquers kingdoms along the Indus Valley.

321–180 BC

Mauryan Empire, including reign of Ashoka (274–236 BC). Spread of Buddhism.

AD 78–200

Gandhara flourishes.

1940

Muslim League demands separate nation of Muslims on subcontinent.

August 14, 1947

Pakistan becomes independent nation, including West and East Pakistan.

August 15, 1947

India becomes independent nation.

October 1947

First war between Pakistan and India over Jammu and Kashmir.

1949

United Nations negotiates cease-fire between Pakistan and India.

1958

Mirza abolishes constitution and declares martial law.

November 1988

Pakistan People's Party wins elections, restores democracy.

December 1988

Benazir Bhutto sworn in as first female prime minister of a Muslim nation.

October 1989

Pakistan rejoins British Commonwealth of Nations.

November 1990

Nawaz Sharif elected prime minister.

April 1993

Sharif government dismissed by president.

October 1993

Benazir Bhutto elected as prime minister for second time.

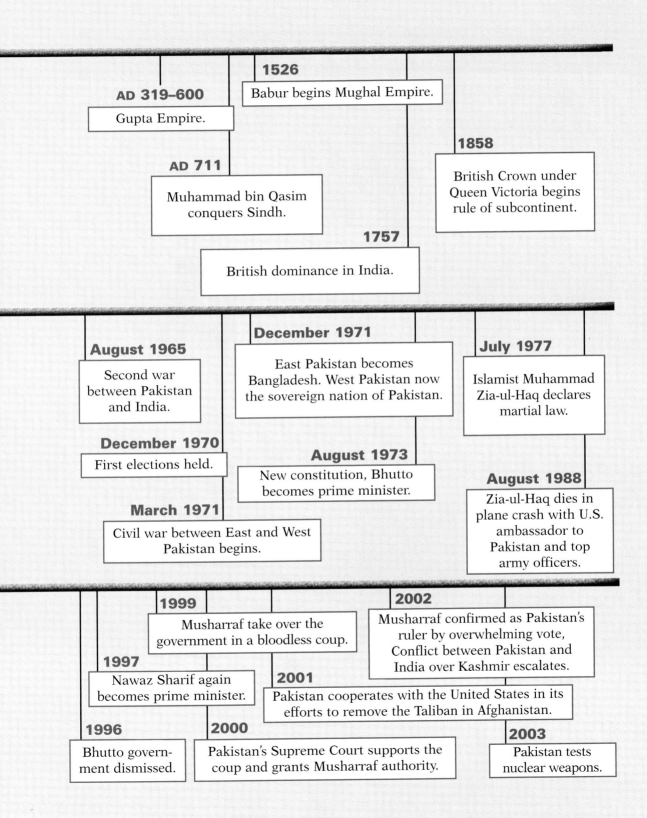

AD 319–600
Gupta Empire.

1526
Babur begins Mughal Empire.

1858
British Crown under Queen Victoria begins rule of subcontinent.

AD 711
Muhammad bin Qasim conquers Sindh.

1757
British dominance in India.

August 1965
Second war between Pakistan and India.

December 1971
East Pakistan becomes Bangladesh. West Pakistan now the sovereign nation of Pakistan.

July 1977
Islamist Muhammad Zia-ul-Haq declares martial law.

December 1970
First elections held.

August 1973
New constitution, Bhutto becomes prime minister.

August 1988
Zia-ul-Haq dies in plane crash with U.S. ambassador to Pakistan and top army officers.

March 1971
Civil war between East and West Pakistan begins.

1999
Musharraf take over the government in a bloodless coup.

2002
Musharraf confirmed as Pakistan's ruler by overwhelming vote, Conflict between Pakistan and India over Kashmir escalates.

1997
Nawaz Sharif again becomes prime minister.

2001
Pakistan cooperates with the United States in its efforts to remove the Taliban in Afghanistan.

1996
Bhutto government dismissed.

2000
Pakistan's Supreme Court supports the coup and grants Musharraf authority.

2003
Pakistan tests nuclear weapons.

PAKISTAN

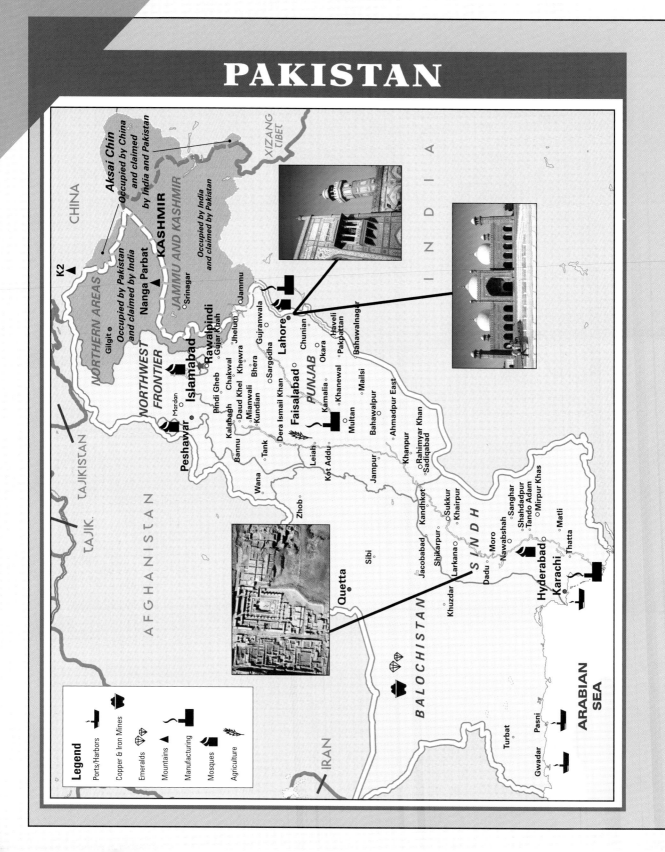

ECONOMIC FACT SHEET

GDP in US$: $282 billion

GDP Sectors: services 49.7%, agriculture 25.4%, industry 24.9%

Land Use: Total area 318,438 square miles (796,095 square kilometers) arable land 27%, irrigated lands 20%, permanent crops 1%, permanent pastures 6%, forests and woodlands 5%, national parks 1.3%

Currency: Pakistani rupee (1 Pakistan rupee = 0.0167 dollars or 60.06 rupees = U.S. $1)

Workforce: Labor force 40 million (agriculture 44%, services 39%, industry 17%)

Major Agricultural Products: Cotton, wheat, rice, sugarcane, fruits, vegetables, milk, beef, mutton, eggs

Major Exports: Cotton, textile goods (garments, cotton cloth, yarn), rice, leather items, carpets, sporting goods, fruits, seafood

Major Imports: Industrial equipment, motorized vehicles, iron ore, petroleum, chemicals, grains, flour, edible oils

Significant Trading Partners: United States, Hong Kong, United Kingdom, Germany, United Arab Emirates, Saudi Arabia, Malaysia

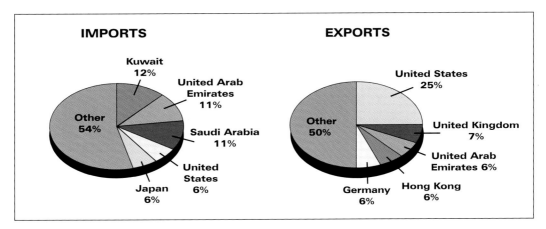

Rate of Unemployment: approximately 6%

Highways: 141,489 miles (228,208 kilometers)

Railroads: 5,440 miles (8,775 kilometers)

POLITICAL FACT SHEET

Official Country Name:
Islamic Republic of Pakistan
(Islami Jamhuria-e-Pakistan)
System of Government: In
transition (formerly a federal
republic, constitution suspended in 1999)
Federal Structure:
Parliamentary form with two
Houses of Representatives,
the Senate (upper house) and
the National Assembly (lower
house). The Senate is a

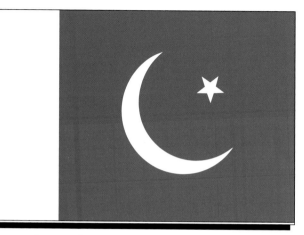

permanent body with 87 members. Members of provincial assemblies from
Baluchistan, Punjab, Sindh and the North-West Frontier Province, and the
Federally Administered Tribal Areas and the Federal Capital elect its members.
The National Assembly has 217 members elected by adults age 18 and older.
Muslims elect 207 members. Members of minority groups elect 10 members. The
members of the Supreme Court are appointed by the president.
Number of Registered Voters: Approximately 72 million in 2002.
National Anthem: "Quami Tarana"
The composition of Pakistan's national anthem is based on Eastern music but
arranged in such a way that it can be easily played by foreign bands. Lyrics were
written by Abul Asar Hateez and the music was composed by Ahmed G. Chagla.
The Pakistani government approved the national anthem in August 1954.

Blessed be the sacred Land
Happy be the bounteous realm
Symbol of high resolve
Land of Pakistan
Blessed be thou citadel of faith

The order of this sacred land
Is the might of the brotherhood of the people
May the nation, the country, and the state
Shine in glory everlasting
Blessed be the goal of our ambition

This Flag of the Crescent and Star
Leads the way to progress and perfection

Interpreter of our past, glory of our present
Inspiration of our future
Symbol of Almighty's protection

CULTURAL FACT SHEET

Official Languages: Urdu, English, Balochi, Sindhi, Punjabi, Pashtun, Saraiki (a dialect of Punjabi), Brahui

Major Religions: Muslim 97 % (Sunni 77 %; Shiite 20 %); Christian 1 %; Hindu 1.5 %; Other (including Sikh) 0.5 %

Capital: Islamabad

Population: 144.6 million

Ethnic Groups: Punjabi 55 %; Sindhi 14 %; Pashtun 9 %; Muhajir 8 %; Baluchi 4 %

Life Expectancy: Males 60.61 years; Female 62.32 years

Time: Pakistan Standard Time is five hours ahead of Greenwich Mean Time

Literacy Rate: Overall 38.9 %; male 55.3 %; female 29 %

National Flower: Jasmine

National Bird: Chukar Partridge

National Animal: Flare-horned Markhor

National Tree: Deodar

National Sport: Field Hockey

Cultural Leaders:
    Painting: Abdur Rahman Chugtai, Iqbal Hussain, Zubeida Agha, Sadequain Naqvi
    Literature: Alamgir Hashmi, Allama Muhammad Iqbal
    Sports: Imran Khan (cricket), Hashim Khan (squash)
    Music: Nusrat Fateh Ali Khan

National Holidays and Festivals

March 23: Pakistan Day (Republic Day)
May 1: Labor Day
August 15: Independence Day
September 6: Defense of Pakistan Day
September 11: Death Anniversary of Muhammad Ali Jinnah

November 9: Allama Muhammad Iqbal Day
December 25: Birth Anniversary of Muhammad Ali Jinnah

Working Life: Among the poorest, laborers, a fourteen-hour day, six days a week is common. In Pakistan, an Islamic nation, people commonly rest on Saturday, though even this is changing.

GLOSSARY

Arabian Sea (ah-RAY-be-an SEE) The northwestern portion of the Indian Ocean, between the Arabian Peninsula and the south Asian subcontinent.

coup d'état (KOO deh-TAH) A French term meaning "blow to the state" that refers to a sudden, unexpected overthrow of a government by outsiders.

caste (KAST) A hereditary social system developed under the Aryan rulers of the south Asian subcontinent as early as 1700 BC. The system established the native peoples as lower class and "untouchable," while the ruling Aryan class became the upper class.

dictatorship (dik-TAY-ter-ship) A form of government in which absolute power is concentrated in one ruler, or in a small group.

exile (EG-zyl) To banish from one's country or home.

forage (FOR-age) To search for food, particularly when food is scarce.

fundamentalism (FUN-duh-MEN-tal-IH-zum) A movement or attitude stressing strict and literal adherence to a set of basic religious principles.

Mesopotamia (mes-uh-puh-TAY-mee-uh) A region between the Tigris and Euphrates Rivers, in modern-day Iraq, which in ancient times was home to great civilizations.

monsoon (mon-SOON) The season in the Indian Ocean area, including the Arabian Sea, marked by heavy rains and high winds.

oppression (uh-PREH-shun) The unjust and cruel use of power to keep people from exercising their human rights; to rule or govern harshly.

pantheon (PAN-thee-on) Those gods that make up a religion where the people believe in more than one god.

partition (par-TIH-shun) A term used for the division of Asian land into India and Pakistan in 1947.

Silk Road (SILK ROAD) A network of trails and primitive roads that connected China and India to the Mediterranean.

-stan Persian suffix meaning land.

FOR MORE INFORMATION

American Institute of Indian Studies
1130 East 59th Street
Chicago, IL 60637
(773) 702-8638
Web site: http://www.indiastudies.org

Asia Society
725 Park Avenue
New York, NY 10021
(212) 288-6400
Web site: http://www.asiasociety.org

Web Sites

Due to the changing nature of Internet links, the Rosen Publishing Group, Inc., has developed an online list of Web sites related to the subject of this book. This site is updated regularly. Please use this link to access the list:

http://www.rosenlinks.com/pswc/paki/

FOR FURTHER READING

Britton, Tamara L. *Pakistan*. Edina, MN: ABDO Publishing, 2002.

Caldwell, John C. *Pakistan*. Broomall, PA: Chelsea House Publishers, 2000.

Kenover, Johnathan Mark. *Ancient Cities of the Indus Valley Civilization*. New York: Oxford University Press, 1998.

Khan, Eaniqa, and Rob Unwin. *Country Insights: Pakistan*. Austin, Texas: Raintree Steck-Vaughn, 1998.

Scarsbrook, Ailsa, and Alan Scarsbrook. *A Family in Pakistan*. Minneapolis: Lerner Publications, 1985.

Sheehan, Sean. *Cultures of the World: Pakistan*. New York: Marshall Cavendish, 1994.

Wagner, Heather Lehr. *India and Pakistan (People at Odds)*. Broomall, PA: Chelsea House Publishers, 2002.

BIBLIOGRAPHY

Adams, Damon. "Putting Some Sparkle in Children's Lives: A Family Physician Builds Schools in Pakistan, Building Hope for a Way Out of Poverty." *American Medical News*, April 15, 2002.

Ahmad, Khabir. "Pakistan's Treatment of Women Criticized." *Lancet*, August 19, 2000, p. 663.

Ahmed, Akbar S. "Pathan." *Encyclopedia of World Cultures. Vol. 3—South Asia*. Paul Hockings, ed. New York: G. K. Hall, 1992. pp. 230–233.

Ali, Ahmed, trans. and intro. *The Golden Tradition: An Anthology of Urdu Poetry*. New York: Columbia University Press, 1973.

Blood, Peter R., ed. *Pakistan: A Country Study*. 6th ed. Washington, DC: Federal Research Division/Library of Congress, 1995.

Edwards, Mike. "Central Asia Unveiled." *National Geographic*, Issue 201 (2002), pp. 108–125.

Edwards, Mike. "Indus Civilization: Clues to an Ancient Puzzle." *National Geographic*, Issue 197 (2000), pp. 108–131.

Elahi, Sarwat S. "Sindhi." *Encyclopedia of World Cultures. Vol. 3—South Asia*. Paul Hockings, ed. New York: G. K. Hall, 1992. pp. 263–264.

Haque, Mohammad Zahirul. "Dr. Abdus Salam: An Intellectual Giant." *Economic Review*, Issue 27 (1996), pp. 45–46.

Hasan, Ijaz ul. "Painting and Sculpture." *Arts & the Islamic World*, Issue 32 (1997), pp. 56–58.

Hashmi, Alamgir. "The Maker of Poems." *World Literature Today*, Issue 71 (1997) Retrieved September 1, 2002. InfoTrac subscription database.

Hashmi, Alamgir. "Pakistan." *Journal of Commonwealth Literature*, Issue 31 (1996), pp. 109–121.

Ingholt, Harald. *Gandharan Art in Pakistan*. New York: Pantheon Books, 1957.

Jain, Sushil. "Hidden in the Lute: An Anthology of Two Centuries of Urdu Literature." *World Literature Today*, Issue 70 (1996), pp. 761–762.

Khan, Adeel. "Pakistan's Sindhi Ethnic Nationalism: Migration, Marginalization, and the Threat of 'Indianization." *Asian Studies*, Issue 42 (2002), pp. 213–229.

King, John, Bradley Mayhew, and David St. Vincent. *Pakistan*. 5th ed. Hawthorn, Australia: Lonely Planet Publication, 1998.

Kurian, George Thomas, ed. *Encyclopedia of the Third World*, 4th ed. Volume II (Guinea to Pakistan). New York: Facts On File, 1992.

Maas, Peter. "Emroz Khan Is Having a Bad Day: Which Is not Unusual, and Helps Explain Why Pakistan's Youth Are Tinder for Islamic Extremism." *New York Times Upfront*, January 21, 2002, pp. 18–22.

McCarry, John. "The Promise of Pakistan." *National Geographic*, Issue 192 (1997), pp. 48–73.

"Musharraf's Move; Pakistan." *The Economist*, January12, 2002.

Nagi, Anis, ed. and trans. *Modern Urdu Poems from Pakistan*. Lahore, Pakistan: Swad Noon Publications, 1974.

Naqvi, Akbar. "Transfers of Power and Perception: Four Pakistani Artists." *Arts & the Islamic World*. Issue 32 (1997), pp. 9–15.

"One Family Divided: In Pakistan, the Clash Between Extremist and Moderate Visions of Islam Can Be Deeply Personal, as the Tale of One Clan Shows." *Time International*, October 1, 2001, p. 38.

Paine, Sheila. *Embroidery from India and Pakistan*. Seattle, WA: University of Washington Press, 2001.

Parker, David L. *Stolen Dreams: Portraits of Working Children*. Minneapolis: Lerner, 1998.

Parpola, Asko. "The Sky-Garment: A Study of the Harappan Religion and Its Relation to the Mesopotamian and Later Indian Religions." *Studia Orientalia*, Issue 57 (1985).

Quraeshi, Samina. *Legacy of the Indus: A Discovery of Pakistan*. New York: Weatherhill, 1974.

Raffel, Burton. "The Poems of Alamgir Hashmi." *The Literary Review*, Issue 37 (1994), pp. 705–710.

Robinson, Neal. *Islam: A Concise Introduction*. Washington, DC: Georgetown University Press, 1999.

Siddiqi, Akhtar Husain. *Baluchistan (Pakistan): Its Society, Resources and Development*. Lanham, MD: University Press of America, 1991.

Siddiqi, Ashraf, and Marilyn Lerch. *Toontoony Pie and Other Tales from Pakistan*. Cleveland, OH: The World Publishing Company, 1961.

SIL International. "Ethnologue: Languages of Pakistan." 2002. Retrieved July 7, 2002 (http://www.ethnologue.com/show_country.asp?name=Pakistan).

Simons, Lewis M. "Kashmir: Trapped in Conflict." *National Geographic*, Issue 196 (1999), pp. 2–29.

Siraj-ul-Haq, ed. *Sind Through the Centuries: An Introduction to Sind*. Karachi, Pakistan: Publicity and Publication Committee, Sind Through the Centuries Seminar, 1975.

Sirhandi, Marcella C. "Painting in Pakistan: 1947–1997." *Arts & the Islamic World*, Issue 32 (1997), 17–32.

Skinner, Todd. "Storming the Tower." *National Geographic*, Issue 189 (1996), pp. 32–51.

Smith, Huston. *Islam: A Concise Introduction*. San Francisco: HarperSanFrancisco, 2001.

PRIMARY SOURCE IMAGE LIST

Page 8: This photograph taken by Paolo Koch depicts the archaeological site of Mohenjo-Daro and its citadel that dates from between 2500-1600 BC. It is located in the Sindh province in Pakistan.

Page 14: This aerial photograph of Mohenjo-Daro (2500–1600 BC) was taken in Pakistan's Sindh province.

Page 15: Saeed Khan took this photograph during a flood in Rawalpindi, Pakistan, after a heavy downpour in 2001.

Page 18: This is a photograph of the archaeological remains of the Kot Diji Fort located in the Sindh province between Ranipur and Khairpur on the eastern banks of the Indus River. Kot Diji dates from between 2500–2800 BC.

Page 19: The dice pictured here were found in Mohenjo-Daro, circa 3000–2000 BC.

Page 20 (top): This is a photograph of a Harappan seal, found in the archaeological remains of the ancient civilization of Harappa now located in Pakistan's Sindh province.

Page 20 (bottom): A statue from the Harappan culture is located at the National Museum of Pakistan in Karachi, Pakistan.

Page 23 (bottom): This bas-relief of Cyrus the Great is located in Pasargadae, Iran, and dates from the Achaemenid period.

Page 24: A Gupta cave painting in Ajanta, India, depicting Prince Siddhartha dates from the sixth century.

Page 25: A marble bust of Alexander the Great dates from 356 BC and is located at the Louvre Museum in Paris, France.

Page 26: This sixteenth-century illustration from the *Baburnama* is housed in the Victoria and Albert Museum in London, England.

Page 27: This painting by Farrukh Beg depicts Akbar entering Surat in the sixteenth century.

Page 28: This hand-colored engraving of Bombay Green is dated 1812.

Page 29: This photograph of Muhammad Ali Jinnah was taken in 1948.

Page 30: Alexander Bassano created this portrait of Queen Victoria in 1886.

Page 31: This is one page from the official document of the Indian Independence Act of 1947 that freed India from British control and separated its lands from the lands that became Pakistan in August of the same year.

Page 35: This contemporary photograph of a Sindhi man was taken in 1976.

Page 37: This contemporary photograph of the road between Islamabad and Peshawar shows modern signage in Pakistan.

Page 42: This fourteenth-century Arabic book illustration depicts an elephant and a hare and is now housed at the Bibliotheque Nationale in Paris, France.

Page 43: This Bronze statue of the Hindu god Siva dates from the sixth century BC and is located at the National Museum of Pakistan in Karachi, Pakistan.

Page 51: This undated painting titled *The Offering of Prophet Ibrahim* represents the Muslim festival of the Feast of the Sacrifice.

Page 57: Franke Keating took this aerial photograph of the Badshahi Mosque (King's Mosque) built in AD 1673. It is located in Lahore, Pakistan.

Page 58: This is a contemporary photograph of an ancient Hindu temple located outside the village of Gori in Pakistan.

Page 59: This second-century stone relief is housed at the Sarnath Archaeological Museum in Sarnath, India.

Page 60: This Mughal miniature painting of Emperor Babur is located at the Musée National des Arts Asiatiques—Guimet in Paris, France.

Page 61: This is an image of a medieval Koran showing it open to a page from the first *sura*, or chapter.

Page 67: This contemporary image taken by Robert Harding shows the famous Badshahi Mosque located in Lahore, Pakistan.

Page 68: This sculpture of a Fasting Buddha dates from the second or third century AD and is located in the Lahore Museum in Lahore, Pakistan.

Page 69: Shah Jehan built Jehangir's Mausoleum, located near Lahore, Pakistan, in 1637.

Page 70: Miniature painting from the *Baburnama* dates from 1530 and is housed at the National Museum of India in New Delhi, India.

Page 71: This photograph from 1993 shows the Faisal Mosque located in Islamabad, Pakistan.

Page 73: The seventeenth-century Wazir Khan Mosque in Lahore was built by Hakim Ali-ud-din, also known as Wazir Khan, governor during the reign of Shah Jahan.

Page 79: This Indian miniature painting from a *Ragamala* book is dated 1660 and housed at the Marco Polo Gallery in Paris, France.

Page 80: This manuscript dates from the sixteenth century and is from an anthology of some famous works of Persian poetry.

Page 81: This text of *Sri Bhagavata Purana* is located at the British Library in London, England.

Page 82: This miniature painting, *Religious Dance of Initiation*, is located at the National Museum of Pakistan in Karachi, Pakistan.

INDEX

Pakistan: A Primary Source Cultural Guide

About the Author

Marian Rengel is a writer and educator living in St. Cloud, MN. She is a faculty member at St. Cloud State University, working in library and technology services. She has been a journalist and a college teacher of English and journalism. Also the author of *John Cabot: The Ongoing Search for a Westward Passage to Asia*, Ms. Rengel is a wife and a mother of two daughters.

Designer: Geri Fletcher; **Cover Designer:** Tahara Hasan; **Editor:** Joann Jovinelly; **Photo Researcher:** Gillian Harper; **Photo Research Assistant:** Fernanda Rocha